31-DAY DEVOTIONAL

SOFTBALL, GLORY & GOD'S STORY

LEAH AMICO

May God bless your
dedication to Him and
protect your softball
playing.

"Big D" and "Bunky"

SOFTBALL, GLORY & GOD'S STORY
31-DAY DEVOTIONAL

ISBN: 978-1722311124

Cover design: Ashlyn Miller

Cover photo credit: USA Softball; Headshot credit: Josh Menashe

Scripture taken from the New King James Version®. Copyright © 1982 by Thomas Nelson. Used by permission. All rights reserved.

Visit my website at www.leah20.com

For information about special discounts available for bulk purchases or for speaking engagement inquiries, contact me at softballglorygodsstory@gmail.com.

Dedication

I dedicate this book to love of my life, my husband, Tommy. Thank you for being the one I can count on at all times. Thank you for your unwavering support on the softball field and in life. You encourage me to step out in faith and follow Jesus wherever He leads. I love you with all my heart and soul.

Acknowledgements

There are many people who have played a role in my faith and my success on the softball field. First and foremost, to Jesus Christ, my Lord and Savior: I will follow You all the days of my life. Thank You for forgiving my sins and for Your gift of eternal life.

To Jake, Drew, and Luke: You boys are God's greatest gifts to me. I am blessed to be your mom, and I pray for you each to follow Jesus with all your heart every single day.

To my mom, Denise DiCrasto: Thank you for always believing in me and allowing me to follow my dreams. Thank you for introducing me to Jesus as a little girl. I love you.

To my dad, Fred O'Brien: Thank you for the countless hours spent practicing with me and coaching me and for loving softball as much as I do. I love you.

To my sister, Amy, my brother, Keith, and your families: Thank you for always supporting me and for the memories we make whenever we are together. To John and Sue Amico: Thank you for being the best in-laws ever. Love you. To Ed, Bob, and John Amico, and your families: I am thankful for you and wish you all lived closer.

To Coach (Mike Candrea): You are truly like a second father to me. I am so grateful God led me to Arizona. You made me a better player and a better person. To all my coaches and teammates throughout my entire career: Thank you for your friendships, your sisterhood, and your impact on my life. I will never forget our times together on the field.

To my Arizona teammates: My four years competing as a Wildcat were some of the best years of my life. You all are a big reason why! To Jenny Dalton-Hill: I am so thankful we were roommates, teammates, and close friends. College would not have been the same without you.

To my Olympic teammates: We were the best in the WORLD! I love you all. To Dot Richardson: I am inspired and encouraged every single time we talk! Thank you for your passion for Jesus. To Laura Berg: I will never forget our memories from being roommates for 10 years on Team USA. Outies Rule!

To my JFSC Crew: My camp devotions are what inspired me to write this book. I cherish our friendships, memories, and so many laughs! To Jennie Finch: Thank you for your friendship and for living out your faith so boldly.

To Julie Reitan: Thank you for sharing the love of Jesus through your actions and your words. I will see you in heaven one day and give you the biggest hug! To Doug and Chloe Gotcher: Thank you for helping me to learn and grow in my walk with Jesus. You are a huge part of my testimony, and I am so grateful for your impact.

To Paula Sommers: I thank God for placing you in my life as a mentor. God knew the perfect timing and the perfect person for me. Love you.

To Kristi Menashe (my best friend): Thank you for all your help looking over this book and editing it with me. Thanks for your friendship. We have laughed together, cried together, traveled together, and learned about Jesus together. To my Bible study girlfriends: You are real, transparent, and make me want to walk in victory with Jesus every single day. I love you all! Thank you for encouraging me throughout this process.

To Patty Gasso: Thank you for your boldness and desire to give God the glory in all you do! Thank you for writing the foreword for my book.

To Kaye O'Sullivan: Your example to me and our talks about Jesus encourage me more than you know. Thank you. To Donna Noonan: I appreciate all you do for women of faith in sports all over this country. Thank you for your friendship.

To Tom Julian: Thank you for helping me turn a desire to write a devotional book into a reality. To Ashlyn Miller: Thank you for using your gifts to create the cover of my book. To Becky Lopanec: Thank you for helping me put the finishing touches on my project. To Keith O'Brien: Thank you for investing so much time on formatting my book for me. To Valerie Wibbens: Thanks for adding a special touch with the artwork.

To all softball players: You are my inspiration. I want you to know how much Jesus loves you. I pray you find your identity in Him alone. I hope you seek God and learn His Word so you can have victory in all you do!

Contents

Foreword

Softball is an unforgiving sport. A .400 batting average is exceptional, yet a hitter is still "failing" 6 out of 10 at bats. The same attitude applies toward defense, as making one error in a game can ruin the rest of your game. A pitcher can throw a pitch out of the strike zone, and it gets sent over the fence. All heads go down in disappointment, and the pitcher wants out of the game. This game is full of emotional ups and downs; but the downs seem to paralyze us.

If we allow it to, softball can dictate our self-worth. Society is so focused on winning in sports that perfection is the expectation, even if it is unrealistic. If you are a winner on the field, you are praised. If you lose, it's doom and gloom and long car rides home. God intended for us to use our athletic gifts to give Him glory regardless of the outcome. He loves me for who I am, not for what I do and how successful I am on the field. In Philippians 4:12-13, Paul preached: "I know both how to have a little, and I know how to have a lot. In any and all circumstances I have learned the secret of being content—whether well fed or hungry, whether in abundance or in need. I can do all things through Him who strengthens me."

There is no one who has played the sport of softball who understands her purpose better than Leah Amico. In *Softball, Glory & God's Story*, Leah will share with you her journey on and off the field. Leah will share her Olympic experiences, as well as different softball lessons learned along the way, and how she relates them to Scripture and biblical truths. Leah has been a significant Christian role model to the softball community, and her experiences will touch your heart and change your life.

Leah's passion for the Lord is infectious, and I wanted her to be part of our team chapel prior to stepping on the field at the Women's College World Series. We are Oklahoma Sooners, and she is an Arizona Wildcat! How can I ask her to do such a thing? No matter the name on front of the uniform or the university we represent—ultimately, we are sisters in Christ, and I wanted our team to witness what passion for our Lord and Savior looks like!

2 Timothy 4:7 reads: "I have fought the good fight, I have finished the race, and I have kept the faith." Leah Amico has fought the fight, had faith through it all, and ultimately, she finished the race. The amazing news is that you get to experience it all in *Softball, Glory & God's Story*.

My prayer for those who read Leah's devotional is that they would allow God to work internally on anything that needs to be given to Him. Leah's investment is a great example of Matthew 5:16: "Let your light shine before men, so that they may see your good works and give glory to your Father in heaven." I see how you shine, Leah! May we all follow your example and allow our lights to shine as well!

Thank You, Lord!

Patty Gasso

Head Softball Coach (University of Oklahoma)

31-DAY DEVOTIONAL

SOFTBALL, GLORY & GOD'S STORY

Day 1

Believe

I was the type of player who always looked forward to practice. I enjoyed working on fielding ground balls and trying to make the hardest plays on defense. I expected to hit line drives during batting practice, and when I failed to accomplish my short-term goals, I would get frustrated.

My high expectations pushed me to work harder until I found a way to achieve success. I focused on the fundamentals of hitting and fielding, and I always kept the standard high. I had some good days and some bad days. I knew my work was never done. After a good day, I had the mindset of finding a way to get even better the next day. Practice was always my preparation, and it was during my preparation that I was building confidence.

I have noticed that many players do well in practice but struggle during a game. They are not able to transfer their confidence from practice to the game. They may struggle because there is added pressure during a game. In practice when you make a mistake, the result does not get recorded. In a game, once a ball is hit and a play is made, the outcome is final. We must have a strong mental approach if we want to be successful when it counts.

As players reach higher levels in softball, mental strength will separate the good from the great. In other words, some players have more belief in themselves than other players do. When we BELIEVE we can accomplish great things, we are one step closer to making it happen.

It is important for us to believe that we can make the defensive play, place the pitch where we want it, hit the ball no matter the movement or speed, or throw the runner out trying to steal second base. Belief impacts our action. Belief puts us on the offensive. When we doubt, we become defensive and fearful. When the pressure mounts, some athletes play to *not* make a mistake rather than confidently approaching each play.

In relation to our faith, belief is crucial. The Bible says if you "confess with your mouth the Lord Jesus and *believe in your heart* that God has raised him from the dead, you will be saved" (Romans 10:9, emphasis mine). So, *belief* is the key to salvation. Since we are saved from eternal death in hell, belief is the essence of life. "The wages of sin is death, but the gift of God is eternal life in Christ Jesus our Lord" (Romans 6:23). Despite being born sinners, destined to die without a Savior, we can gain eternal life through faith (or belief).

Once we recognize who we are, as sinners, our belief in Jesus and the choice to follow Him changes everything. We are promised a relationship with Jesus Christ both now on earth and eternally in heaven, and belief is the pathway to both. The word the Bible uses for "believe" means "to be convinced of something." As we are convinced that Jesus Christ died and rose on the third day, we must acknowledge and accept that He did it for us, conquering sin and death. If we confess our sins, we find that Jesus is faithful and just to forgive us and purify us from all unrighteousness (1 John 1:9).

The word believe also means to trust. We trust Christ to save us; we are not saved by any good works on our part. When our belief in Christ turns into action, we experience victory in areas of doubt, fear, and temptation because God supplies us with His power.

God gives us an incredible example of His victory when we have doubt. Martha, Mary, and Lazarus were very close friends of Jesus. Lazarus had died, and Martha was grieving. She was filled with sadness, anger, and doubt. Just before He raised her brother, Lazarus, from the dead, Jesus told Martha, "Did I not say to you that if you would believe you would see the glory of God?" (John 11:40). She thought all hope was gone...but she was wrong.

Jesus Christ can change any situation. Don't doubt your abilities, and don't doubt what God can do in your life. He can bring the dead to life, so he can meet any need in yours. Remember Jesus' own words: "all things are possible to him who believes" (Mark 9:23).

"Jesus said to her, 'I am the resurrection and the life. He who believes in Me, though he may die, he shall live. And whoever lives and believes in Me shall never die. Do you believe this?'" -John 11:25-26

"These are written that you may believe that Jesus is the Christ, the Son of God, and that believing you may have life in His name." -John 20:31

Prayer

Dear God, help me to trust You completely. Remind me of Your promises when I start to doubt. Help me to walk in confidence on and off the field. Amen.

Today's Bible Reading: John 11:1-44

Your Story. . .God's Glory

1. Do you perform better in practice or in a game? Why do you think this happens?

2. Do you believe you can make the big play to change the game for your team? Why or why not?

3. Have you placed your complete trust in Jesus Christ and asked Him to set you on the path God has chosen for you? If you haven't done this, what's stopping you?

Day 2

Leadership

No matter what position we play, where we are in the batting lineup, or what level of softball we are fortunate enough to participate in...to compete, succeed, and win, every team must have leaders. Whether they are coaches that work with us on fundamentals and manage the game on our behalf, or they are leaders on the field who are peers: leaders are pertinent to the game!

How a coach treats and speaks to her players, other coaches, and even umpires, matters. How a coach views his competition or his players on the field matters. If the coach views things negatively, the team simply will not respond as a unit and winning will become much more difficult.

As competitive softball players, we need leaders who are confident and positive. Leaders must be able to keep the team intact—even during a mid-season slump. They must convey to each and every player just how important they are to the team and to one another. The Bible is filled with amazing stories of how important leadership is.

In the book of Numbers, Chapter 13, God spoke to Moses, the man He had chosen to lead the Israelites. God told Moses to send out twelve spies to look at the land of Canaan. God had promised the land to the Israelites! It was a land flowing with milk and honey. It was also a land that produced much fruit. However, the Bible also tells us that the people who dwelled in the land were strong, and the cities were secured and well protected (Numbers 13:28).

What happened?

The twelve spies went out, but when they returned, TEN of them focused on the difficulties of taking over the land more than on God's promise to give it to them.

Ten out of the twelve!

One of the twelve—a man named Caleb—understood and believed in the promises that God had spoken. He said, "Let's go take the land, for we are able to overcome it" (Numbers 13:30). Even as the other ten continued to be negative, Joshua (also one of the twelve) agreed with Caleb. Joshua spoke up and said, "The land is exceedingly good land. If God delights in us, then He will bring us into this land and give it to us, a land which flows with milk and honey. Only do not rebel against the Lord, nor fear the people of the land...their protection has departed from them, and the Lord is with us. Do not fear them" (Numbers 14:7-9).

Fearing the people was not the answer. Trusting God was the answer!

Think about playing in a game—where seven out of the nine players on the field don't believe they can win the game because their opponent is in first place, is faster, and has a higher batting average. What do you think their chances are to beat this team if only two players believe they can win? Not very good! Let's choose to be like Caleb and Joshua. Let's believe we can have success no matter how high the odds are stacked against us.

As God's children, we can go out every day and compete on the field. We can trust that no matter what happens, God is with us. We can always learn a lesson—in both the good times and the bad. The key is to stay positive. We must never play out of fear. We need to move forward boldly and stay aggressive. We must ask God to do a work in and through us. When we play this way, we will begin to lead by example and others will want to follow.

"Remember those who rule over you, who have spoken the word of God to you, whose faith follow, considering the outcome of their conduct." -Hebrews 13:7

"But without faith it is impossible to please Him, for he who comes to God must believe that He is, and that He is a rewarder of those who diligently seek Him." -Hebrews 11:6

Prayer

God, I pray that You will give me courage to stand up for what is right and to speak Your truth no matter what other people think. Help me to see things from Your perspective and to know that my strength comes from You. God, make me a better leader on and off the field. Amen.

Today's Bible Reading: Numbers 13:17-33; 14:1-10

Your Story. . .God's Glory

1. What are some opportunities that God has given you to be a leader?

2. How can you lead with faith and positivity?

3. How can you play with confidence instead of fear?

Day 3
Suit Up

Each time we head out to the field to compete in a softball game, we need to make sure we are wearing the correct uniform and are using the proper equipment if we want to be successful.

In softball, our uniforms and equipment include:

•jersey- with our name and number for identification

•cleats- for firm footing

•glove- to handle anything hit our way

•helmet- to protect us in the batter's box

•bat- to hit the ball being thrown by the pitcher

Without these "tools" it would be impossible to play, compete, bat, or field. Each piece is designed to help us play the game that we love.

The Apostle Paul wrote about something similar in Chapter 6 of Ephesians. He called it: "The Armor of God."

Just like the items mentioned above for softball, Paul knew firsthand what was needed to effectively walk, talk, and live the Christian life. He wrote...

"Therefore, put on the full armor of God, so that when the day of evil comes, you may be able to stand your ground, and after you have done everything, to stand. Stand firm then, with the belt of truth buckled around your waist, with the breastplate of righteousness in place, and with your feet fitted with the readiness that comes from the gospel of peace. In addition to all this, take up the shield of faith, with which you can extinguish all the flaming arrows of the evil one. Take the helmet of salvation and the sword of the Spirit, which is the word of God" (Ephesians 6:13-17, NIV).

As Christians, we need to "put on" this armor daily. Just as we have been provided the gear that we need for our games, God provides the proper armor to live in His will. It is important for us to wear it each and every day—knowing the truth, reading His word, and seeking to have our faith increased so we can stand against all that Satan throws at us. All the while, we should seek nothing more in our lives than pleasing and obeying God and our Savior, Jesus Christ.

What helps us in our daily battles as Christians is "suiting up." We "wear" our armor, and nothing can make us stronger than that! Knowing His truth and living in obedience to God's ways brings about victory in our lives.

How free do we feel when we get to step out onto that softball diamond to play the game that we love? How confident do we feel after we have put in the time to practice, practice, practice?

God's truth propels us toward the same freedoms and confidence when we obey Him.

When I dressed in my uniform, grabbed my glove, and took the field, I was ready to compete. I was confident because I had the proper gear and equipment. Whether it was fielding or hitting, I was prepared.

The more we know God's Word, the more we read it, the more we pray, the better equipped we will be when the time comes for us to be in a position to use it. Let's put on that armor and let's fight the good fight!

"Therefore let us cast off the works of darkness, and let us put on the armor of light. Let us walk properly, as in the day. But put on the Lord Jesus Christ." -Romans 13:12-14

"Be renewed in the spirit of your mind, and put on the new man which was created according to God, in true righteousness and holiness." -Ephesians 4:23-24

Prayer

Lord, teach me how to put on the armor of God every day. I know I need to read the Bible daily in order to be ready for the battles I will face. God, help me to stand firm and be strong in my faith. Amen.

Today's Bible Reading: Ephesians 6:10-20

Your Story. . .God's Glory

1. In what ways do you prepare for a game?

2. What piece of the armor of God do you struggle to put on daily, and how can you change that?

3. How can you begin and end your day in the confidence that comes from Christ?

Day 4

Set An Example

The tryout we had all been waiting for was finally here.

It was September, 1995, and the tryout for the first ever Olympic softball team was under way in Oklahoma City. Think about how important this day was for women in sports. There were 67 women from all over the United States, all different ages, and all different levels of experience who were invited to this tryout. At the end of the tryout, only 15 team members and five alternates would be selected to represent the United States of America in softball at the Atlanta 1996 Olympic Games.

This would truly be an honor for me and so many other women. We went through a lot of different workouts, drills showing off our skills, conditioning, and testing. The second half of the tryout was set up for us to scrimmage each other and compete against all the athletes trying out for a spot on the Olympic team.

Emotions were running high for everyone. Many women had put their lives on hold waiting for the opportunity to have a chance to make an Olympic team. I was in college at the time and was honored to be trying out for a spot.

I can remember overhearing some of the older athletes, women in their late twenties and early thirties, talking about how the players with more experience should be the ones named to the team. I was one of the younger athletes at the tryout, and I remember feeling like age should not be the main factor and that it should be based on ability. I believed that having the most talented, well-rounded team, regardless of age, was the key to winning the gold medal.

The Bible also mentions youth and reminds us that God does not discriminate based on age. He will use everyone, young or old, who is devoted to accomplishing His will. The Bible says, "Let no one despise your youth, but be an example to the believers in word, in conduct, in love, in spirit, in faith, in purity" (1 Timothy 4:12).

Nobody should ever use their age, or youth, as an excuse. Even if others think you are too young to accomplish great things, you should not listen to the negativity that it could produce within you.

Remember, with God all things are possible (Matthew 26:19b).

God calls every one of us to follow Him wholeheartedly and to know Him by learning His Word. When we do this, we can live out the command in 1 Timothy 4:12 to be an example in conduct, love, faith, and purity.

I ended up making the team at 21 years old, and we even had an 18-year-old high school senior on the team. Our team won the gold medal that year with a good combination of both younger talent and veteran leadership.

Whether you are trying out for a team or are a veteran on a team, remember to stay focused on what you are trying to accomplish. You should never let the opinions of others get in the way of the goals you are working toward. Put in the hard work and leave the results up to God. His plans for our lives are always better than our plans!

"Let no one despise your youth, but be an example to the believers in word, in conduct, in love, in spirit, in faith, in purity." -1 Timothy 4:12

"For my thoughts are not your thoughts, nor are your ways my ways,' says the LORD. 'For as the heavens are higher than the earth, so are my ways higher than your ways, and my thoughts than your thoughts.'" -Isaiah 55:8-9

Prayer

Dear God, I trust Your plan for my life. I will give my best at everything I do. Keep me from comparing myself to others or making excuses. Help me to be an example to those around me. Amen.

Today's Bible Reading: 1 Timothy 4:12-16

Your Story. . .God's Glory

1. What experiences have you had where you felt your youth was looked down upon?

2. In what ways is God using you to be an example to your teammates and peers in word, in conduct, in love, in spirit, in faith, or in purity?

Day 5

Perspective

My college team had just picked up an important win. Though we won by a large margin, I walked off the field frustrated and discouraged because I had a really bad game offensively. I didn't feel as if I had contributed at all to the team win. But then, I looked up into the stands and there, smiling from ear to ear, was one of our biggest fans—Steven.

Always faithful to our team, Steven, a young man in his thirties, never missed a game. He was constantly there cheering us on. Steven always wore a smile, despite the fact that he was wheelchair bound (due to an accident from his younger years). Whenever I walked up to him after a game, Steven would give me a high five and would tell me that I played well. He was always so happy to watch our team compete.

As discouraged as I was that day, my perspective suddenly shifted as soon as I saw Steven's smile. There I was, totally down on myself, frustrated about having had a bad game, and yet, God (through Steven) showed me that I needed to learn to be grateful. God impressed upon my heart in an instant that I should be thankful and appreciative of the fact that I was physically capable of playing the game I love. My identity was never intended by God to be found in what I accomplished or achieved on the softball field. I finally understood that my identity was to be found in Jesus Christ alone.

This is one of the most amazing things about our Savior: if we allow Him to, He brings people and circumstances into our lives to remind us of what is truly important.

Every day is a gift from God. By allowing Him to guide us in softball and in our lives, all that He brings about will—without a doubt—have a positive effect on us and on those around us.

Our hearts will change and become more thankful.
Our confidence will grow.
Our willingness to grow as a teammate will emerge.

That night, I went home and opened up my Bible to the book of Ecclesiastes. As I read this book, written by Solomon (the wisest man to ever live on the earth!), it gave me even more perspective on my feelings about the game. As Solomon was searching for what mattered most, he had come to the conclusion that "everything was meaningless." By itself, that statement seems harsh. Solomon shares what he learned and why he felt that way throughout Ecclesiastes.

Near the end of the book, Solomon wrote, "Let us hear the conclusion of the whole matter: Fear God and keep His commandments, for this is man's all. For God will bring every work into judgment, including every secret thing, whether good or evil" (Ecclesiastes 12:13-14). Even though Solomon was the wealthiest king in his lifetime, he realized that riches and titles were not what mattered most. Living a life set apart for God is what matters most!

We can find ourselves chasing after so many things, but in the end, they are really meaningless. Things like: finding our identity in our success, tying our worth to how many likes or followers we have on social media, trying to fit in and be popular, worrying about our looks, or caring too much about what other people think about us. Instead, we should be focusing on God's truth and who He says we are as His children.

Solomon's words reminded me that even on the field, as I went out to be my very best—softball is still a sport. It should be fun, and it can teach us so many life lessons, but it should not cause us to be burdened and stressed out all the time. When we lose perspective, God will give us reminders—like when I saw Steven and was immediately grateful to be able to play this game.

We can chase after success and awards, but those things will never fulfill us. The only thing that will satisfy and fulfill every person is a relationship with God and living for His glory!

"Rejoice always, pray without ceasing, in everything give thanks; for this is the will of God in Christ Jesus for you."
-1 Thessalonians 5:16-18

"For our light affliction, which is but for a moment, is working for us a far more exceeding and eternal weight of glory, while we do not look at the things which are seen, but at the things which are not seen. For the things which are seen are temporary, but the things which are not seen are eternal." -2 Corinthians 4:17-18

Prayer

Thank you, Lord, for the opportunity to play the sport of softball. Help me to keep everything in perspective no matter what happens on the field. My desire is to be thankful for all You have done in my life. Amen.

Today's Bible Reading: Ecclesiastes 3

Your Story. . .God's Glory

1. Is your identity in Jesus or are there things that threaten to take His place in your heart and mind? Take a moment to reflect and pray. Write down your thoughts.

2. Perspective, peace, and satisfaction come from keeping God first. List the things that threaten to knock God out of the number one spot in your life? (Below is an example of a prayer you can pray, asking God to help you to keep Him as the priority in your life.)

Prayer

Dear God, the things I just listed are things that I think about and care about. But, they are not more important than my relationship with You and knowing You. Please give me wisdom, Lord Jesus, to pursue You first and to give You glory as You write my story.

Day 6

Conquerors

It was a warm afternoon in the fall of my freshman year at the University of Arizona, where I was recruited from high school as a pitcher and first baseman. We were scrimmaging against our teammates, and I still remember the lesson I learned that day. The hitter, who everyone knew was one of the most potent offensive threats in the entire nation, was up to bat.

It was an intense and competitive moment even though we were teammates. There were seven other teammates on the field, but as soon as I received the signal for the pitch, the focus was on me, the pitcher, and my catcher competing together against the batter. I gripped the seams of the softball, took a deep breath, and went into my pitching motion.

I snapped my wrist at my release point to get as much movement on the ball as possible. The pitch was a screwball. As a lefty, this pitch was usually effective against right-handed hitters because the ball spins and breaks away from them. The ball was spinning toward the intended target, the outside corner of the plate, where the catcher's glove was set up to receive the ball. I saw the batter throw her hands and the bat at the ball and *bam!* The catcher and I watched the barrel of the bat connect, sending the ball flying a great distance over the left field fence.

Immediately, I was deflated. My heart sank and I was upset.

My catcher came out to talk to me. She could see that I was discouraged, and she told me it was not a bad pitch. She reminded me of who the opponent was: that she was on our side—that she was our teammate. In that moment, I was thankful that I was on her team and did not have to face her in a real game.

Now, as many of you know by now, I am competitive! You have to be competitive to be successful in college softball and in the Olympics.

Internally, I was discouraged and had been questioning myself. *Did I have what it took to compete at this level on such an elite college team?*

I realized that I needed to use that situation to gain a more resilient mindset. I needed to find a way to "toughen myself up" mentally, so that the next time I was in that type of situation, I could deal with it in a better way.

In softball, we will experience many highs and lows. It is normal to feel discouraged when things don't go the way we want them to, but if we can learn from our experiences, we will become better athletes.

The Bible says that we will have trials and hard times in life. In fact, Jesus Himself said to His disciples, "In the world you will have trouble. But take heart! I have overcome the world" (John 16:33).

Some people go through challenges and become bitter while other people go through trials and become better. The Bible says that nothing can separate us from the love of Christ. In fact, Paul writes that tribulation, persecution, famine, sword, and more cannot separate us from the love of Christ (Romans 8:35-39). Not even death can separate us! The Bible goes on to say that even in the hardest of circumstances, "we are more than conquerors through Christ who loves us" (Romans 8:37).

More than conquerors! That means we have victory even when we feel down.

We must always remember: no matter what challenges we face, no matter the mistakes we have made, no matter how discouraged we get...if we have placed our trust in Jesus, then His love is enough to give us victory at all times.

"Yet in all these things we are more than conquerors through Him who loved us." -Romans 8:37

"But may the God of all grace, who called us to His eternal glory by Christ Jesus, after you have suffered a while, perfect, establish, strengthen, and settle you." -1 Peter 5:10

Prayer

Please remind me, Jesus, that I am more than a conqueror when my feelings tell me otherwise. Give me Your perspective regarding my circumstances. Keep my eyes and heart focused on You and Your love for me. Amen.

Today's Bible Reading: Romans 8:31-39

Your Story. . .God's Glory

1. Can you remember a time where you felt discouraged or defeated?

2. What can you do in those types of moments to be reminded that you are more than a conqueror?

3. Are you becoming bitter or better through your trials?

Day 7

Trust

The 1999 Pan American Games in Winnipeg, Canada was the big tournament of the summer. Over 5,000 athletes from 42 nations in 35 different sports converged on this one place to compete. It is held one year before the Olympic Games and for me, it was a couple months prior to the try out for the USA Olympic Softball team. The team selected would compete in the 2000 Sydney Olympic Games.

This added a whole new level of stress and expectation.

I was playing right field and batting in the lower part of the lineup. When I got up to the plate in the first game, my fundamentals were all off. I wasn't seeing the ball well, and I was off balance in my stance.

In softball, to hit the ball well, you need to have a good foundation; there are so many things that have to be in unison to effectively hit a softball that drops, curves, or rises while traveling at a high speed from a short distance away.

I was frustrated with myself after the game, and I knew I had to figure something out quickly, but I didn't have time to practice. Practice was where I gained my confidence and was what I relied on for preparation. Even though I knew what I should have been doing as a hitter mentally, physically it was not happening.

From that point on, I began to recite the Bible verse Joshua 1:9 in my head. It says, "Have I not commanded you? Be strong and courageous. Do not be afraid; do not be discouraged, for the LORD your God will be with you wherever you go."

I knew that if I became discouraged at this time, my results would only get worse in the games. Instead, I mentally competed at the plate and started telling myself that I was better than the pitcher I was facing. I was trying to focus on the ball being thrown and not worry about what was happening with my body positioning physically.

It worked! I took a more aggressive approach than I normally would and hit some hard line drives into the right-center and left-center gaps in the outfield. I produced extra base hits at a time where I could have gone into a slump. Staying positive mentally and remaining focused on the truth that God was with me helped me to have success offensively.

Out in right field, as I would get into my ready position for each pitch, I was reciting the verse, Joshua 1:9, over and over to myself. I was prepared and ready for the ball. I wanted the ball to be hit my way so I could make a play.

Having that verse to rely on reminded me that God was with me, even in the frustrating, discouraging, and hard times. After that week, I knew I would never forget the words in Joshua 1:9. This verse became more than just words to me on that softball field in Winnipeg, Canada. I experienced God's promise of being with me right where I was. I felt God's peace in the midst of competition. God wants you to experience His peace and presence as well!

We ended up beating Team Canada in the championship game to win the gold medal at the 1999 Pan American Games, and I finished the tournament much better than I started it. I accomplished my goal of giving my very best on that field and trusting God with the results.

You can always have courage and strength because God keeps His promises!

God will be with you at all times; no matter where you have been, what you have done, or where you are going. Remember His command: do not be afraid, and do not be discouraged, for He is always with you.

"Have I not commanded you? Be strong and of good courage; do not be afraid, nor be dismayed, for the LORD your God is with you wherever you go." -Joshua 1:9

"Fear not, for I am with you; Be not dismayed, for I am your God. I will strengthen you, Yes, I will help you, I will uphold you with My righteous right hand." -Isaiah 41:10

Prayer

Your Word reminds me that You are always with me, God, wherever I go. Thank You for Your faithfulness. Please give me strength and courage in every battle I face. Amen.

Today's Bible Reading: Joshua 1

Your Story. . .God's Glory

1. What thoughts go through your head when you are struggling in practice or in a game?

2. What verse(s) can be an encouragement to you in times of frustration or fear? (Check out: Jeremiah 29:11, Psalm 55:22, Isaiah 40:31, Galatians 6:9)

3. Recall a time when you relied upon God's strength and knew He was with you.

Day 8

A Changed Life

I remember it as if it were yesterday...

At the time, I was in college. Earlier that day, I attended my classes and softball practice. I was exhausted, but I had promised my teammate, Julie, that I would attend a sports ministry meeting. To be honest, I would have much rather stayed home relaxing, but I had given her my word—and so I went.

That night, with other athletes in attendance, the leader of the ministry, Doug, started to talk about the Trinity: God the Father, God the Son, and God the Holy Spirit, and how God is three persons in one.

This was not an easy concept for me to understand. Even though I was tired, I listened intently as Doug spoke about the different roles each has. God the Father sent His Son, Jesus Christ, to die on the cross for all of our sins. It is through the blood that Jesus shed on the cross and the power of God that raised Him from the dead that we are offered eternal life. Once we place our trust in Jesus, the Holy Spirit enters into our lives. In the Bible, the Holy Spirit is described as a "Counselor" who will help guide us every day (John 16).

As I listened, I soon realized that though I believed in God, I did not know who He truly was. Everything was foreign, but soon God started to give me a deeper understanding, and it was after that meeting that my life changed.

That fall night back in 1995, I asked God to forgive me of my sins and asked Jesus Christ to come into my heart.

I was convinced. I wanted to follow Him. I wanted to know God the Father, God the Son, and God the Holy Spirit.

To receive Jesus Christ, we first need to recognize that we are all sinners. We must ask Him to forgive us by repenting, or turning from our ways to God's way. We then profess Jesus Christ as our Lord and Savior. "Everyone who calls on the name of the Lord will be saved" (Romans 10:13).

Once we are saved, the Holy Spirit dwells inside of us and will guide us into all truth (John 16:13). Jesus says the Holy Spirit will comfort us when we are hurting (John 14:27) and will make us aware of any sin in our lives (John 16:8). The Holy Spirit also helps us to pray when we don't know what to say (Romans 8:26).

I immediately recognized the work of the Holy Spirit in my life. I noticed how some of my thoughts were changing. God was opening my eyes to things I thought were "good," but in reality, the Bible was teaching me that they were not good. I found true purpose in my life for the first time.

As a competitive softball player, I recognized that my growth and improvement on the field came through my years of hard work in practice and competition. I began to understand that I should be growing as a Christian as well. Growing up, I had hoped I was good enough to go to heaven, but I was not growing in my faith because I did not have a personal relationship with Jesus. I realized I gained my views about God from opinions around me rather than from the Bible. As I began to attend more sports ministry meetings and ask questions, I learned how to find the answers in God's Word.

Slowly, my life started to change, and I felt exactly what Paul, the Apostle, felt when he wrote, "Therefore, if anyone is in Christ, he is a new creation; old things have passed away; behold, all things have become new" (2 Corinthians 5:17).

"If you confess with your mouth the Lord Jesus and believe in your heart that God has raised him from the dead, you will be saved." -Romans 10:9

"He who has received His testimony has certified that God is true. For He whom God has sent speaks the words of God, for God does not give the Spirit by measure. The Father loves the Son, and has given all things into His hand. He who believes in the Son has everlasting life; and he who does not believe the Son shall not see life." -John 3:33-36a

Prayer

Jesus, I am a sinner in need of your forgiveness. Thank You for dying on the cross for my sins. I need You to change me from the inside out. Please help me to grow in the knowledge and wisdom of God. Amen.

Today's Bible Reading: John 3

Your Story. . .God's Glory

1. Have you made the life-changing decision to accept Jesus Christ as Lord and Savior today (or in the past)? If so, write about your experience.

2. What changes has the Holy Spirit made within you?

3. Is there someone you know who is in need of the Savior? Pray for them today and seek opportunities to share with them.

Day 9

Diversity

Out of all of the women invited to the tryout, only fifteen athletes were selected by USA Softball's selection committee to the first ever Women's Olympic softball team in 1996.

We all came from different backgrounds, had different belief systems, different heights and body types, and our ages ranged from 18 years old to 34 years old. Each one of us brought different strengths to the team and had a role to fulfill and a position to play.

In the Bible, Paul mentions the "body of Christ" (followers of Jesus) and compares it to a human body. He brought up a great question. Paul asked, "If the whole body were an eye, where would the sense of hearing be?" (1 Corinthians 12:17). Paul names other body parts as well—ears, hands, feet—to show how each part is important and has a specific role. The same can be said of the players on the field for softball.

If all fifteen of us on our team were pitchers, the team would not have been very good because we would have been lacking in all the other positions. If everybody was a power hitter, we wouldn't have the speed needed at the plate to get on base and score runs. Each role and position on the field and in the hitting lineup is unique. Every role is important, even if a player is a substitute and not a starter.

We had fifteen players on our team and yet, only nine were in the lineup at any given time. We were all different types of athletes with different roles, yet we had one unified goal and that was to bring home the gold medal for the United States of America. We wore one uniform, and every player's job was to do her part and to build upon what her teammates were doing.

This is so important for all of us to know—these differences were the key to our success as a whole.

This is how it is in the kingdom of God. We all have different strengths and we each matter in the family of God. The Bible tells us that there are diversities of gifts, distinct roles we play, and different areas where God uses us, but it is the same God who is working in all these differences.

When we allow God to guide our lives, God will show us the gifts and roles He has created us for. There is nothing more exciting than following God's leading. You may be tested and challenged, but God will show you His faithfulness as you lean on Him. It is important to be connected to the body of Christ, other Christians, because we are here to encourage each other—just like we find encouragement on our teams. We can lift each other up when things get tough, and we can celebrate together when things go well.

We are all invited to be on one team, God's team, representing Jesus Christ. When we start following Jesus, our goal should be to draw as close as possible to Him. The only way this can happen is if we consistently read, learn, and apply God's Word to our lives. Then, God will start to change us from the inside out. As we start to change, we can encourage others by letting them know that God made them unique for a reason and has a plan for their lives as well. We should celebrate the fact that we are all different, yet all made in the image of God.

"There are diversities of gifts, but the same Spirit. There are differences of ministries, but the same Lord. And there are diversities of activities, but it is the same God who works all in all." -1 Corinthians 12:4-6

"But God composed the body, having given greater honor to that part which lacks it, that there should be no schism in the body, but that the members should have the same care for one another. And if one member suffers, all the members suffer with it; or if one member is honored, all the members rejoice with it." -1 Corinthians 12:24-26

Prayer

Thank You, God, for making me unique. I now see how being different is a positive thing. Please give me opportunities to encourage others. Remind me that every role matters and is important. Amen.

Today's Bible Reading: 1 Corinthians 12

Your Story. . .God's Glory

1. What strengths has God given you as a softball player?

2. How have you seen the differences of your teammates contribute to the success of the team?

3. What are some ways you can use your strengths to encourage your teammates?

Day 10

Underdog

It was my freshman year in college, and I was standing on the biggest softball stage at the time; my team made it to the championship game of the 1993 Women's College World Series.

Our opponent was UCLA, the school that was known for having a softball dynasty. This school had this reputation because they held the most national titles out of any collegiate team, and to top it off, their senior starting pitcher was one of the best players in the world. We batted first. Our leadoff hitter slapped the ball to the shortstop, and the ball was overthrown. It went flying past the first baseman, allowing our first batter to reach safely. The next hitter in our lineup hit a ground ball to the second baseman, and our runner advanced to second base.

It was now my turn up to bat. The ball was being thrown up to 70 mph! Believe me—that is fast! I quickly fell behind in the count—no balls and two strikes. After battling and fouling off multiple pitches both in and out of the strike zone, I connected with a ball low in the zone and hit a line drive up the middle past the pitcher. The centerfielder caught the ball after one hop and fired home.

Even though the ball beat our runner to the plate, she made a beautiful slide around the catcher and tagged home plate with an outstretched hand. She was safe, and we led the game 1-0. We had to battle for seven innings, but we held onto the lead and won 1-0. We were National Champions!

We were the underdogs in that game—and what's more amazing is that we won even though our team only had one hit in the entire game. My hit was the only hit allowed by UCLA's pitcher, but it was the winning RBI to help us win the championship! We kept UCLA from scoring—the Bruins only had two hits of off our All-American pitcher, and our defense made great plays behind her.

It reminds me of the story of David and Goliath. Goliath was a Philistine giant that hated God's people and was expected to take down any opponent he faced. Not only that, he spent every day teasing and taunting the people of Israel. David was an unlikely hero and did not have the size, strength, armor, or sword to match up against Goliath. However, David believed in the power of His God. With faith, he chose to stand up against the enemy of Israel. He used a sling and a single stone to take down the giant and brought victory to his people.

When we know that God can use every single one of us, we can be ready for any challenge. It is not always the teams or people that everyone expects to win that have the final victory. But in order to have victory, we have to be willing to battle like David did. When Goliath was causing fear in the Israelite camp, it showed that they were looking at the enemy and not trusting in what God could do through them.

David had experienced God's power and strength because he was close to God. As He trusted God completely, he saw God work in his life. This helped him to have confidence against this giant when everyone else was running away in fear.

As a child of God, we have access to God's strength, hope, peace, courage, and confidence. We can overcome any obstacle and we can face any challenge head on, just like David. Our victory is always found in Jesus Christ.

With God, even the most unlikely person can become a hero.

"Then David said to the Philistine, 'You come to me with a sword, with a spear, and with a javelin. But I come to you in the name of the Lord of hosts, the God of the armies of Israel, whom you have defied.'" -1 Samuel 17:45

"But thanks be to God, who gives us the victory through our Lord Jesus Christ." -1 Corinthians 15:57

Prayer

Dear Jesus, thank You for reminding me of the victory I have in You. I can face any obstacle, no matter how big, with confidence because You are on my side. Amen.

Today's Bible Reading: 1 Samuel 17

Your Story. . .God's Glory

1. What experience(s) have you had where you were the underdog?

2. When you come up against a "Goliath" in softball or in life, how can you remind yourself to trust in God's power to help you overcome your challenge?

3. What's a current fear or struggle of yours that can be faced by battling in prayer?

Day 11

Follow

I was fortunate to play for positive, knowledgeable, and encouraging coaches at every level of softball. I always wanted to do well, so I listened to my coaches and took the advice they gave me.

This is very important for everyone to do. I can remember when I first learned the importance of listening to my coaches. It was when I was a young pitcher taking private lessons. By listening to my pitching instructor and doing what he asked of me in regard to mechanics and my mindset, I became more accurate with locating pitches in specific locations and increasing my speed by a few miles per hour.

As a hitter, I listened to what my coaches told me to do and made adjustments with my swing. This helped me to hit the ball consistently with more power. I saw my batting average go up, and I was on base a lot more often. In college and on the Olympic team, our coaches gave us instructions less frequently, but they still pointed out any bad habits they saw in our fundamentals. There were only minor adjustments that needed to be made, but even at our level, we were still listening to our coaches and applying what they told us to work on. My coach could see what I sometimes couldn't feel in my mechanics. When I made adjustments according to this advice, the results were always positive.

The Bible tells us that God has given all followers of Jesus a Helper called the Holy Spirit. It says that the Holy Spirit will teach us all things and bring to our remembrance all things that Jesus said in God's Word (John 14:26).

As softball players, we need to be coachable. We first have to listen to and learn from our coaches, and then we can remember what they have taught us and apply those principles on and off the field. It's the same when we follow Jesus. We read the Bible so we can learn what God wants to do in our hearts and lives.

The Holy Spirit will make us aware of sin in our lives when we get off track by bringing conviction. This means that in our consciences and thoughts we will know when we are going against God's ways. We sin when we violate God's laws. Some examples of sin are: hatred, anger, sexual impurity, envy, lying, jealousy, gossiping, and selfish ambition.

Romans 3:23 says that "all have sinned and fall short of the glory of God." This means that we are not alone in our struggle to always do what is right in God's eyes. In fact, it is impossible to never sin. But with God's help, we can sin less and walk in righteousness.

This became possible because God sent His Son, Jesus Christ, to die for all of our sins (past, present, and future). Jesus shed His blood and gave up His life on the cross because of His great love for us. When Jesus rose from the grave, He conquered sin and death and is alive forevermore. God sent the Holy Spirit to live inside of His followers from that point on. Once we place our trust in Jesus as our Lord, we become righteous in God's eyes.

God desires for us to be filled with the "fruit" of the Holy Spirit— displaying characteristics like love, joy, peace, patience, and kindness. But, we must be willing to respond when God shows us our weaknesses and choose to do what is right. Fortunately, God promises to help us if we will just ask Him.

God will always teach us more when we are willing to listen and obey. Listening to our coaches helps us to have success on the field. Obeying God's commands and responding to the leading of the Holy Spirit brings victory in every area of our lives.

"But the Helper, the Holy Spirit, whom the Father will send in My name, He will teach you all things, and bring to your remembrance all things that I said to you." -John 14:26

"But the fruit of the Spirit is love, joy, peace, longsuffering, kindness, goodness, faithfulness, gentleness, self-control. Against such there is no law." -Galatians 5:22-23

Prayer

God, thank You for the gift of the Holy Spirit in my life. Forgive me of my sins. I desire to be more like Jesus. Help me every day to obey Your commands in the Bible so I can live a life that honors You. Amen.

Today's Bible Reading: John 14

Your Story. . .God's Glory

1. Have you asked Jesus to come into your life? If yes, how has the Holy Spirit been working in you?

2. Which fruit of the Spirit listed in Galatians 5:22-23 is the hardest for you to live out and why? Which is the easiest?

Day 12

True Strength

I experienced a lot of success with the teams I competed for throughout my career. I remain thankful for the coaches who helped me become a better athlete. I am grateful for my teammates who pushed me to always strive to meet higher expectations. The higher the level of softball I competed in, the greater the challenges and the harder I pushed myself.

On the USA Olympic team, my teammates had amazing talent, strength, and speed. We spent hours on the field working on fine-tuning our skills (throwing, fielding, hitting, and pitching). Countless hours were also spent working on team defense, offensive strategies, and intersquad scrimmages. We focused on our strengths, individually and as a team. Speed, agility, weights, and conditioning were other important components of our training.

I worked as hard as I could in my training, and yet I was not able to lift as much weight as most of my teammates. In fact, when our team was tested for grip strength, the results showed that I was the weakest player on the team in that category. I would never had made the Olympic weight lifting team, but in softball I was successful despite my "weakness" in grip strength. We should always work to improve our weaknesses, but we must focus on using our strengths to be successful.

The Bible teaches us that God is our strength. When we trust in Him and rely on Him, He will give us the strength needed in any areas where we are weak. In the book of Judges (Chapters 13-16), we learn about the life of Samson, the strongest man in the Bible.

Samson was chosen and set apart by God from birth. He became the fifteenth judge of Israel, and he fought the Philistines while helping to deliver God's people. Samson fell in love with a woman, Delilah, who was paid by the Philistines to find out where his strength came from. Their goal was to make him weak and overtake him.

At first, Samson would not reveal the secret of his great strength. But over time, Delilah wore him down with her repeated requests until Samson gave in and told her that it was his long hair that made him strong. As part of a vow, his hair was never to be cut with a razor. Samson's enemies, the Philistines, used this knowledge to subdue him. They cut off his hair while he slept, and he lost all of his strength. Next, they took him prisoner, gouged out his eyes, and forced him to grind grain.

The Philistines brought Samson into their temple to watch him perform. He asked his captors to let him lean against the supporting pillars to rest. He prayed one more time asking God for renewed strength. God answered his prayer. Samson used his strength to break the pillars, causing the temple to collapse, killing him and his enemies inside.

Samson had supernatural power from God, but all of us are promised God's "strength" to get through each day. We need spiritual strength, hope when we are discouraged, perspective when we are struggling, and faith when we are feeling depressed. We can trust God's promises and walk in joy and victory. Call out to God and find the strength that only He offers.

My weakness did not keep me from winning gold medals. In the same way, our weaknesses and struggles will never keep us from experiencing God's best for our lives. Every day we must turn to God and ask Him to help us and to be our strength. God will take our weaknesses and show us that His strength is enough for us.

"The Lord is my strength and my shield; my heart trusted in Him, and I am helped; therefore my heart greatly rejoices, and with my song I will praise Him." -Psalm 28:7

"He gives power to the weak, and to those who have no might He increases strength." -Isaiah 40:29

Prayer

In my weakest moments, God, remind me that You are near and that Your strength is always available. As I read the Bible, help me to meditate upon Your promises because I can always count on You. Amen.

Today's Bible Reading: Psalm 28

Your Story. . .God's Glory

1. What are a few of your strengths and weaknesses?

2. Think about a time when you felt weak. Did you rely on the Lord for strength?

3. Does it bother you to think of yourself as being weak and needing His strength, or does it help you to feel safe and secure?

Day 13

Focus

It was a warm, sunny day as I watched the opposing team take the field for their pre-game warm ups. Each player took her position, the coach had a bat in her hand, and the players were ready for the ball to be hit.

But, I noticed something missing.

The coach was not holding a softball. The coach pretended to toss a ball up and swung her bat through the air. Even though there was no softball, the left fielder went through her fielding position and her throwing motion as if she caught and threw the ball. The second baseman pretended to receive the phantom ball from the left fielder, and this is how they took an entire pre-game warm up. There were some "plays" made at the fence and even some fake diving catches.

The players were cheering and excited the entire time. They looked like they were making great plays, but they really weren't because there was no ball to reveal if those plays could actually be made. This team was missing the main thing, the ball.

This is not reality in softball. If there is no ball, there is no game. The softball is the focus at all times. You should always know where the ball is when playing. You need to stay focused and keep your eyes on the ball if you want to hit, field a ground ball, or catch a fly ball. In fact, as a hitter, you want to learn how to read the spin on the ball out of the pitcher's hand. This takes deep concentration and focus as the pitcher reaches her release point in her motion—and we all have seen what happens when a fielder pulls up her glove on a ground ball before it reaches her glove. When we are careful to keep our eyes set on the ball until the play is complete, we will have more success.

The Bible teaches us that Jesus is and should be the main focus for Christians. Jesus Christ is what sets Christianity apart from all the other religions in the world. It is Jesus who was God in the flesh when

He walked this earth. Jesus did this, so we can have a relationship with God and have abundant life (John 10:10b). And, it is Jesus who loves us unconditionally and helps us when we need it most.

When we draw near to Jesus, we realize that we don't have to try to be good enough. We can stop pretending that we have it all together when we are struggling. When we turn to Jesus, we can be assured that we are never alone. Knowing Jesus means understanding there is a purpose for our lives.

Too many people are missing out on someone very special—and His name is Jesus—because they look to religion or good works in order to get to heaven. Jesus said, in John 14:16, "I am the way, the truth, and the life, and no one comes to the Father except through Me."

We no longer need to pretend we have it all together. We can seek the One who has the answers to life's questions. We can experience the love of God in Jesus Christ today.

"I have come that they may have life, and that they may have it more abundantly." -John 10:10b

"Jesus answered and said to her, 'Whoever drinks of this water will thirst again, but whoever drinks of the water that I shall give him will never thirst. But the water that I shall give him will become in him a fountain of water springing up into everlasting life.'" -John 4:13-14

Prayer

Jesus, You are everything to me. I know You offer the abundant life that I desire. Thank You for loving me unconditionally. Help me to draw near to You. Amen.

Today's Bible Reading: John 1:1-18

Your Story. . .God's Glory

1. If somebody asked you who Jesus Christ is, what would you tell them?

2. What is the difference between following a religion and having a personal relationship with Jesus Christ?

3. Have you made a commitment to follow Jesus?

Day 14

Give Your Best

I was fortunate to play a lot of different positions throughout my career (pitcher, outfield, first base). In the 1994 Women's College World Series, I was playing center field when I made an important out. We were playing against a very strong Fresno State team. The hitter in the batter's box was one of the best in the country and was known for her power. As the pitch was thrown to her, she connected with the ball, and it was heading straight towards me. As it sailed high in the air, I knew it was over my head, so I turned back and started sprinting toward the outfield fence.

The ball was hit so hard that I didn't think I had a chance to catch it. As the ball was just passing over my head, I extended my arm out as far as I could while jumping in the air at the same time. The fence came up to the middle of my back, and I was bending halfway over the fence backward when the weight of the ball hit the leather pocket of my glove. The momentum of my feet coming to the ground brought me forward and back into play.

What would have been a home run became a crucial out for our team. My pitcher was so excited that she sprinted all the way from the pitching circle to centerfield to give me a hug, even though it was only the second out of the inning.

A photographer was able to catch the progression of my catch on her camera. When I saw the final picture, I had to laugh. There were people holding up their hands celebrating, thinking it was a home run. Some fans were moving out of the way in the bleachers behind me thinking they were going to get hit. Others were reaching forward trying to catch a home-run ball.

But instead of a fan catching a home run ball that day, I ended up with the ball in my glove. If I had given up and not given it all that I had, the results would have been different. I never would have known I could make that play if I did not try (picture on page 134).

We don't always know how things are going to turn out, but with God, anything is possible. When we obey God and commit to learning God's Word, we can be ready for God to work in ways that we don't even know are possible. When people went to Jesus for healing, many miracles were performed.

Jesus brought sight to the blind, health to the sick, life to the dead, and a voice to the mute. These people woke up needing a healing touch and met the Healer that day. We have access to Jesus at all times.

When we get tested, or stretched to our limits, we must not lose our faith. We need to trust that God will work together all things for our good (Romans 8:28). If a friend betrays our trust, if a relationship falls apart, if our family is going through conflict, or if we just can't keep up with the expectations of others, God is there to help us.

We should give our best no matter what we are doing. We must persevere when we feel overwhelmed in school or overmatched in competition. When we give our best, we just might make the play that everyone thinks is impossible, and God will use it to show us how much we really can do through Christ.

"And we know that all things work together for good to those who love God, to those who are the called according to His purpose." -Romans 8:28

"And whatever you do, do it heartily, as to the Lord and not to men, knowing that from the Lord you will receive the reward of the inheritance; for you serve the Lord Christ." -Colossians 3:23-24

Prayer

God, I am thankful that I can call out to You at any time, and You will hear me. Please work together all things in my life for good like Your Word says. I love You, God. Amen.

Today's Bible Reading: Matthew 9:18-38

Your Story. . .God's Glory

1. What is a big defensive play or game defining hit you have made in the past?

2. How has your faith been tested?

3. Where do you need God to step in and bring help or hope?

Day 15

Ambassadors

Every softball team has uniforms that they wear when they are competing in a game.

The jersey shows which team they are representing.

Being on the United States Olympic Team was the biggest honor I had in softball. Wearing the USA jersey was a dream come true. I wanted to represent our country well. Through our success, our team brought attention to the ability we possessed. How we celebrated and treated our opponents showed our character. Our standard was to always have integrity and class whether we were on or off the field.

This integrity didn't start once I made the Olympic Team. It was instilled in me long before I made it to the big stage in softball. My parents showed me how to win and lose with grace. My expectations were to work my hardest and earn a position on a team. It was never expected for a spot to be "given" to me.

I was taught to respect my coaches and follow their instructions. It was not acceptable to bad mouth the coaches because I didn't get to play the position I wanted to play. I learned the importance of being a good teammate by encouraging others and always putting the team above myself. These are skills that translate into everyday life. It is about doing what is right more than what feels best for yourself. The example of living this way impacts everyone around you.

Putting others above yourself can be hard. God loves us and wants us to look out for the interests of others and love our "neighbors" (or teammates) as ourselves. There are many Bible verses about being humble and not trying to exalt ourselves. This is hard to do because we are constantly told to do whatever it takes to be the best without regard for others. When God is leading you, you can work to be your best in a way that honors Him. God will exalt you, or lift you up, in His own way.

The Bible refers to all followers of Christ as ambassadors. An ambassador is someone who is a representative. Just like I was an ambassador for USA Softball, you are an ambassador for your team. All who follow Jesus are considered ambassadors for a bigger purpose, God's glory. The Apostle Paul said that we are ambassadors, as though God was making His appeal through us (2 Corinthians 5:20). This means that God is using us as examples for other people, so they will want to know God too.

As an ambassador on the field, I was able to show people that I played for God by how I responded in my struggles and in my success. I tried to be an example and continued to support my teammates when I played poorly. I felt grateful for my success and thanked God for my talent when I performed well. I added a Bible verse after my name when I signed autographs for fans while playing for Team USA so people would know I played for God.

It is easier to be good examples when things are going well for us, but when we start to struggle on the softball field, fight with our friends, or get jealous of others, we sometimes act in ways that we regret. Let's remind ourselves that we are ambassadors for God, even on the softball field. In fact, when you ask for God's help to be a good example anytime things go wrong, people will notice, and you can tell them that God is helping you to represent Him well.

"Now then, we are ambassadors for Christ."
-2 Corinthians 5:20a

"Let nothing be done through selfish ambition or conceit, but in lowliness of mind let each esteem others better than himself. Let each of you look out not only for his own interests, but also for the interests of others."
-Philippians 2:3-4

Prayer

Dear Lord, I am honored to be an ambassador for Christ. Keep me focused and humble. Use me for Your glory, God. Thank You for all You have done in my life. Amen.

Today's Bible Reading: 2 Corinthians 5:12-21

Your Story. . .God's Glory

1. What are some ways you can be an ambassador for Christ to your teammates or the people who watch you compete?

2. What areas do you struggle in when things don't go your way, and what can you do to try to change?

Day 16

The Narrow Way

Run 60 feet and turn left.

That is what you do when you hit the ball. We all had to learn that there was only one direction to run the bases. Most of us have seen little ones just starting out who hit the ball and take off running toward third base. Usually there is a coach running after them and redirecting them in the correct direction toward first base. Sometimes young players will miss a base and quickly learn that they can't advance until they touch each base; and the only way to get home is to touch first, second, and third base.

God's Word teaches us that there is only one way to heaven. It is through His Son, Jesus Christ, and the blood He shed on the cross for our sins. If there was another way, God would never have allowed Jesus to go through so much pain, suffering, and death.

The good news is that Jesus conquered death when He rose from the dead on the third day. It seems easy—just follow Jesus and He'll get you to heaven, but we learn in God's Word that it's not as easy as it seems. Jesus told us in Matthew 7:13-14 that most people don't believe He is the Savior of the world and others don't want to follow Him. He said there is a narrow gate that leads to life, but only a few find it. And there is a wide gate that leads to destruction and many enter it.

In order to win the game in softball, you must score more than the opposing team. In order to get to heaven, we must enter the narrow gate, and that means placing our trust in Jesus as Savior and Lord. We must recognize that we are sinners who can't get to heaven apart from faith in Jesus.

In softball, we work to become better. With God, we must remember we can't work our way into heaven. Our works do not gain us favor with God, but instead show that we are following Jesus.

God's Word makes it clear: if we love Him, we will obey His commands. Let's read God's Word every day so we can know what those commands are. Let's pray and ask God to help us to obey Him in every area of our lives.

The narrow way is the harder way. Making it to the championship game, being the most valuable player, or getting the college scholarship is also a narrow path. The narrow path means more dedication, more time commitment, and more sacrifice. The results will reveal who has chosen to take the narrow road to achieve greatness. It is hard, but it is always worth it.

The narrow way with Christ is the only way we find true victory in life. We must be committed, dedicated, and focused on Jesus, and He will help us stay on course.

As we walk through the narrow gate, we can help others to find the path that will lead them to Jesus, the only One who can offer eternal life.

"Enter by the narrow gate; for wide is the gate and broad is the way that leads to destruction, and there are many who go in by it. Because narrow is the gate and difficult is the way which leads to life, and there are few who find it."
-Matthew 7:13-14

"For this is the love of God, that we keep His commandments. And His commandments are not burdensome. For whatever is born of God overcomes the world. And this is the victory that has overcome the world—our faith." -1 John 5:3-4

Prayer

God, please help me to stay on the narrow path that leads to life even when it is not popular. I want to be set apart for You. I commit my life to following You wherever You will take me. Amen.

Today's Bible Reading: Matthew 7

Your Story. . .God's Glory

1. What are some signs showing that you have chosen to take the narrow road to be your best on the softball field?

2. What are some actions and choices you have made that show you have chosen to follow Jesus through the narrow gate?

Day 17

The Mental Game

See the ball, hit the ball, and keep it simple.

Take a deep breath. Relax. Keep your eyes on the ball. Stay aggressive. Lay off bad pitches. Have quick hands. These are some of the things we think about as hitters. These are also the tips we hear during the game from our coaches on the field or our parents in the stands. There can be so many things to think about when you step up to the plate. But when a hitter is at her best, she is relaxed, has a clear mind, and is seeing the ball well.

The best hitters have a plan when they hit. You should also have a plan when you step into the batter's box. As the pitcher goes into her windup, do your best to clear your head, focus on the pitcher's release point, and react to the pitch that is thrown. Easier to say, harder to accomplish. This is why the best athletes take so many swings in practice. They are training themselves for the game when they will most likely have only two or three at bats.

Some players can easily clear their heads in practice, but the fear of failure causes them to overthink during a game. Other players have too many thoughts running through their minds because they can hear their parents yelling from the stands. Fear of failure can paralyze hitters to the point that they freeze up and don't swing even though a strike is thrown.

The opposite can happen as well. If a hitter feels outside pressure to be more aggressive, she may be more likely to swing at pitches nowhere near the strike zone. Both actions lead to poor results. The key is to learn how you react in game situations and train in a way that prepares you for success even when under pressure. Once you learn how best to clear your mind and stay calm in the batter's box, your body will be relaxed, and you become more likely to hit the ball hard and have quality at bats.

Confidence is the most important part of the mental game. If we want to play well, we need to stay positive mentally and believe in ourselves. A good way to build confidence is to think about times that you have been successful in the past. When you recognize negative or fearful thoughts, quickly replace them with truth. When I played, it helped me to recite a Bible verse in my head whenever negative thoughts crept in.

A verse that reminds us to stay confident and not be fearful is 2 Timothy 1:7. It says, "For God has not given us a spirit of fear, but of power and of love and of a sound mind." We can face any challenge sent our way because we have a God who has given us a spirit of power, love, and a sound mind. We fight fear with faith. Even when we fail, we keep fighting. We keep believing. In time, we will see that a positive mental approach will improve our play on the field. But, we must train our minds.

Training our minds can help us off the field as well. As much as we athletically train in our sport, we need to equally train our minds to know and understand God's Word. As we "train" consistently by studying and memorizing scripture, we will be equipped with God's promises when fear or doubts creep in. Knowing, believing, and living out God's truth will lead to experiencing God's peace, love, hope, and joy in all areas of our lives. Understanding what God says about us will give us true and lasting confidence and will remind us of our purpose.

Remind yourself that God has given you a spirit of power and love and not a spirit of fear. He is there to help you focus on good things and not dwell on negative thoughts. Ask God to guide you when you go out to practice or a competition. Then go out, stay mentally strong, leave everything on the field, and play with nothing to lose.

"For God has not given us a spirit of fear, but of power and of love and of a sound mind." -2 Timothy 1:7

"Finally, brethren, whatever things are true, whatever things are noble, whatever things are just, whatever things are pure, whatever things are lovely, whatever things are of good report, if there is any virtue and if there is anything praiseworthy–meditate on these things." -Philippians 4:8

Prayer

Dear God, please help me to push out any negative thoughts in my head. I want to think about whatever is true. You have given me a spirit of power and of love and of a sound mind. Keep my mindset positive on and off the field. Amen.

Today's Bible Reading: Proverbs 2:1-9

Your Story. . .God's Glory

1. What are some negative thoughts you struggle with on the softball field?

2. What positive words or verses can you focus on when negative thoughts arise?

3. Write down one of the adjectives listed in Philippians 4:8 that you want to focus on, and ask God to help you apply it to your thought life.

Day 18

Teamwork

The best teams usually have more than talent alone—they also have good chemistry.

Getting along well with each other, respecting your teammates, and encouraging other players are often key components of having a championship team.

Each of us has the choice to be a good teammate or not. In team sports, the success of the team will only happen with unity among and within the group. When individuals start to care more about their own success or playing time than the good of the team, problems start to arise. When players become selfish, the team suffers.

To be a good teammate, you need to think about your attitude, your behavior, and your reactions to your teammates and coaches. You should be happy for your teammates when they play well, even when you are in a slump. When a teammate makes an error on the field, you should be the first one to encourage her and tell her you believe in her. If you are struggling on the field, you need to stay focused and not let your emotions control you. When you are a substitute player, you need to support the girls on the field and be ready to enter the game at any time. These are the actions of a player who wants what is best for her team.

The example of Jonathan and David, in 1 Samuel 18 & 19, is a great reminder to all of us to be supportive of our friends and teammates.

Jonathan was King Saul's son, who befriended a shepherd boy, named David. David became well known after he killed Goliath, a Philistine giant. Though Jonathan should have been the likely heir to his father's throne, God chose David to be the next king of Israel. Jonathan could have been jealous and turned on David. Instead, he protected him from harm and spoke well of him. Jonathan also "stripped himself of the robe that was on him and gave it to David, and his armor, and even his sword and his bow and his belt. And David went out and was successful wherever Saul sent him" (1 Samuel 18:4-5a). Jonathan gave up his own gear because he knew David needed it for battle.

David's success was a result of Jonathan's support. Jonathan helped David because he cared more about his friend than he did about having power or position. In the same way, we should treat all of our teammates with kindness and want to see them to succeed.

A team will always benefit from having players who are willing to sacrifice for the sake of what's best for the team. This means cheering for a teammate even when you are having a bad game. It means supporting a teammate who plays your position even when she gets the starting role over you. When you have a team full of encouraging players, team chemistry will naturally happen.

David never forgot the kindness Jonathan showed to him. Your teammates will never forget the kindness and encouragement you give to them either.

"Two are better than one, because they have a good reward for their labor. For if they fall, one will lift up his companion." -Ecclesiastes 4:9-10a

"And let us consider one another in order to stir up love and good works, not forsaking the assembling of ourselves together, as is the manner of some, but exhorting one another, and so much the more as you see the Day approaching." -Hebrews 10:24-25

Prayer

Lord, thank You for my teammates. Let my words and actions toward them show Your love. I want to be supportive and encouraging to them. Amen.

Today's Bible Reading: 1 Samuel 19:1-7

Your Story. . .God's Glory

1. What qualities do you think make someone a good teammate?

2. Name a couple of ways you can support your teammates and friends.

Day 19

Maturity

Fundamental skills are the foundation for all softball players. Throughout every level of play, athletes work on fielding and hitting mechanics. Besides learning the physical part of the game, we also must learn the rules and strategies of the game.

I started playing softball when I was six years old and didn't retire until I was 29 years old. Even after playing for over twenty years, I continued working to become a stronger player. Each year, as I practiced, trained, and competed, my expectation was to become a better athlete, both mentally and physically. This only happens when we spend time perfecting our skills and training to improve. As we understand the game better, we become more likely to anticipate what will happen and execute the plays that need to be made. Our confidence will build as we experience success. All of this leads to us becoming more mature as athletes.

We should always be learning, growing in experience, and improving our strength as we continue in this sport.

The same is true for us as Christians. We should not be the same from the first year we are a Christian to the next year, and the year after that. God loves us as we are and wants everyone to draw near to Him. But, He also loves us so much that He would never leave us as we are. God wants us to become who He has created us to be. When we surrender and draw near to God, He will change us from the inside out. This is a process and it takes time, but there will be growth as we study the Bible and apply it to our lives.

I continued to learn and mature as a softball player until the day I retired. It's the same in our faith. No matter how long we have followed God, we can always learn more about Him. I accepted Jesus a long time ago, but I still have a lot of growing to do. Every single day, I need God's strength to change any thoughts or actions of mine that do not honor Him. I strive to follow Him with all my heart, and yet, I stumble and mess up. I am thankful for the grace God offers to all of His children when we sin. I know any good in me is the result of God working in my life. I will never come to a point in my life where I know all there is to know about God. Nobody will.

All Christians need to grow, or mature, in their faith. Just as babies drink milk and move onto solid food, we start out as "spiritual babies" and grow from there. We won't mature as Christians if we don't read God's Word consistently.

When we first start reading the Bible, it can be very hard to understand. I remember opening God's Word and wanting to learn, but everything seemed so confusing to me. I slowly learned how to understand the Bible by going to church, attending Bible study, and asking people questions who knew the Bible well. My life began to change as I started to apply what I was learning. God can do the same thing in your life as you read His Word and follow Him.

As athletes, we need coaches and teammates around us to help us get better. As Christians, we need spiritual mentors and friends who are willing to help us learn more about God. As we grow in our faith, we become stronger and more spiritually mature; and with growth comes opportunities to show that we are not where we used to be.

Let's not be satisfied with knowing only a little bit about Jesus and God's Word. Let's ask God to help us to learn as much as we can each and every day.

"As you therefore have received Christ Jesus the Lord, so walk in Him, rooted and built up in Him and established in the faith, as you have been taught, abounding in it with thanksgiving." -Colossians 2:6-7

"He who has begun a good work in you will complete it until the day of Jesus Christ." -Philippians 1:6

Prayer

As I read the Bible, God, open my eyes to see and my mind to understand what I am reading. Help me to grow daily in my relationship with You. Please surround me with people in my life who will help me know You more. Amen.

Today's Bible Reading: Ephesians 4:17-32

Your Story. . .God's Glory

1. What are some fundamental truths found in the Bible? (Check out: Ephesians 2:8-9, John 3:16, John 14:6, Romans 10:9-10)

2. Name some ways that show you are maturing in your faith.

Day 20

Prayer

Each team has their pre-game rituals. One of my college teammates started a new one on our team during my senior season. She would head down the line before the game started and would invite everyone on the team to join her in prayer. A handful of players accepted the invitation and joined her in a huddle. As we circled up, we bowed our heads and listened as she prayed to God.

She talked to God so effortlessly. I didn't even know how to pray, or at least that's how I felt. She always knew what to say as she prayed for protection and thanked God for the opportunity to play this sport. I couldn't help but notice that she talked to God like she was talking to a friend. I left the huddle with a desire in my heart to be able to pray with the same confidence and boldness she possessed.

A few games later as we traveled to play, I noticed a paper titled "The Competitor's Prayer" taped to the wall in the dugout. I began thinking about how I could try to memorize the lines and lead our team in prayer. That thought quickly faded as I realized this prayer was way too long, and I am not good at memorizing anyway.

This desire to pray out loud would grow in me until the final game of the season. As soon as we won the game, I asked the team to gather around home plate. With tears in my eyes, the words flowed out of my mouth. I thanked God for these teammates of mine who had become like sisters. All I wanted to do was lift up the name of God on that softball field.

This was the first time I ever prayed out loud in a group. As I shared straight from my heart, I understood the importance of talking to God in prayer naturally and not worrying about having to say the right thing. I wasn't concerned about what others around me thought, and I wasn't trying to impress anyone with my words. My focus was on praising God for who He was, thanking Him for the opportunity to play this sport with these teammates by my side, and giving Him the glory for our victory.

I learned through that experience what prayer is. It is sharing our thoughts, questions, and desires with God. It's crying out to Him when we need Him most. It's asking Him to speak His truth into our lives and trusting that He will reveal Himself to us. It's communicating with the Almighty God who knows us personally and cares about the details of our lives.

My teammate talked to God like He was her friend because she prayed regularly. She knew that God hears the prayers of His children. Her close relationship with God gave her the courage and confidence to ask my teammates and I to join her in prayer before our games. God used her boldness to impact me in a powerful way. God can use you too!

It is important to understand there is no perfect prayer or set way to pray. We just need to be real and have the desire to call out to God. The more comfortable I became in my prayer time alone with God, the more confident I was that one day I could also pray out loud with my teammates.

We all can come before God and pray in Jesus' Name, believing that our Father in heaven hears our prayers and will answer our requests according to His perfect will. Have you prayed before? If not, today is a great day to start.

"Lord, teach us to pray." -Luke 11:1b

"Now this is the confidence that we have in Him, that if we ask anything according to His will, He hears us."
-1 John 5:14

Prayer

Jesus, help me to grow in my prayer life. Teach me how to pray. Help me to spend time talking to You in prayer. Give me confidence to pray with others if this is Your will. Amen.

Today's Bible Reading: James 5:13-18

Your Story. . .God's Story

1. What is your pre-game ritual with your team?

2. Would you consider leading teammates in prayer before a game? If not, why?

3. What are some things you are currently praying for or would like to start praying about?

Day 21

Accountability

I was down in the fielding position. My glove was open, and I was ready to catch the ball rolling toward me. My eyes remained focused on the ball, my feet were firmly planted, and my fundamentals were solid.

The next thing I knew, the ball bounced off the tip of my glove and rolled away from me. I had the choice to hustle, pick up the ball, and see if I still had a play, or to let my frustration get the best of me and give up. I chose to hustle and secure the ball in my glove.

My job was to complete the play and get the ball back to the pitcher. I told myself I would get the ball the next time it was hit my way, refusing to dwell on the error I just made. I wanted a chance to redeem myself, so I was mentally ready to field the ball with focused intensity.

The truth is, everyone makes mistakes at times. We practice and work hard to minimize our mistakes. The real issue is what we do after we make a physical error or a mental mistake on the field.

When we acknowledge the mistake and take a positive mental approach, our opportunity for future success rises significantly. When we refuse to be accountable and make excuses, we hurt ourselves and our team. No one likes to make mistakes on the field, but it happens to even the best players in our sport.

In life, we also mess up at times, and the Bible calls this sin. Some examples of sin in the Bible are: lying, hatred, jealousy, envy, gossip, and stealing. We are not alone in our struggle to do what is right. Every person on earth sins and falls short of the glory of God (Romans 3:23). We all need a Savior. We all need forgiveness.

I thought I was a pretty "good" person when I was growing up. The problem was that I focused on the people around me and compared my choices to their bad choices. This comparison made me feel like I was not as bad as they were. I also believed that I was in good standing with God because I did more good deeds than bad. Once I learned what sin was according to the Bible, I realized I wasn't as good as I thought I was. I immediately recognized my need for the Savior, Jesus Christ.

Our job is to recognize our sin and admit it to God. The Bible teaches us a powerful truth about what happens when we confess our sins to Jesus. 1 John 1:9 says, "If we confess our sins, He is faithful and just and will forgive us our sins and purify us from all unrighteousness." This is a promise. Forgiveness from Jesus is always guaranteed to God's children as we acknowledge our wrongdoing and turn to Him for help.

In contrast, if we refuse to acknowledge our sin, we will not be able to draw near to God (Psalm 66:18). In fact, according to the Bible, we are deceived and the truth is not in us if we say that we have no sin in our lives (1 John 1:8). It is the Holy Spirit who brings conviction to our conscience when we make bad decisions. Let's ask God to help us recognize and turn from any sin in our lives so we can be close to Him.

A coach knows that a player who refuses to be accountable for her mistakes will most likely make the same mistakes again. God knows that we will continue to stumble if we won't admit our sin. Moving forward starts with recognizing where change is needed. Let's be accountable. Accountability sets us up for success on the field and in life!

"God is our refuge and strength, a very present help in trouble." -Psalm 46:1

"Let us therefore come boldly to the throne of grace, that we may obtain mercy and find grace to help in time of need." -Hebrews 4:16

Prayer

Dear God, help me to recognize any sin in my life and confess it to You. I want to honor You in all areas of my life. Thank You for Your forgiveness and for loving me unconditionally. Amen.

Today's Bible Reading: 1 John 1

Your Story. . .God's Glory

1. How do you respond when you make a mistake in a game?

2. How do you feel about the fact that all people sin and need God's forgiveness?

3. Take time to reflect on any sin you have felt convicted over, and pray to God for forgiveness and freedom over that sin.

Day 22

Setting Goals

Winning three Olympic gold medals was something I wouldn't have believed I was capable of doing when I was a little girl.

Three different times, in three different countries, my teammates and I stepped up onto the gold-medal podium and had beautiful, ribbon-laced gold medals placed around our necks.

These medals represented years of practice, games, tournaments, and travel. They represented goals achieved and new levels of success attained along the journey. The medals also represented overcoming obstacles and pushing through slumps. Without dedication, commitment, sacrifice, and hard work, becoming a three-time gold medalist would not have been possible. By setting challenging but achievable goals for myself throughout my career, my goal to represent the USA eventually became a reality.

Goal setting is important for athletes. I want to encourage you to set goals so you have something specific to strive for. If you want to get better at hitting, you can set goals like working toward only swinging at strikes or hitting the ball hard up the middle. If you are a catcher, your goal might be to prevent any passed balls during a game. The goal for your team could be to make it to the playoffs or the championship game. Setting goals can help you to stay focused and to evaluate areas where improvement is needed. We should train and prepare with our goals in mind.

When I was younger, my goal as a pitcher was to throw breaking pitches to specific locations and to keep the opposing hitters from scoring. Offensively, my plan was to have quality at-bats and make solid contact with the ball. I also had the goal of making the all-star team in the early stages of my career. After winning my first national championship at the age of fourteen, my biggest goal was to receive a college scholarship. With hard work in the classroom and on the field, I accomplished that goal by receiving a scholarship to play at the University of Arizona.

The Bible also talks about setting goals. In the book of Philippians, the Apostle Paul spoke about forgetting what was behind him and straining toward what was ahead. He said he wanted to press on toward the goal and win the prize of God's heavenly calling in Christ Jesus (Philippians 3:14). Paul's supreme goal in life was to deepen and broaden his relationship with God. This should be what we strive for as Christians, as well. This only happens when we recognize that we are sinners, place our faith in Jesus, and learn who God is by reading His Word.

Paul knew that the prize for following God with all his heart was to know Christ fully. Paul went through many hardships, trials, and difficulties, but he never stopped giving his all for Jesus Christ. He had accomplished a lot, yet he remained committed to sharing God's truth with as many people as possible. Paul's spiritual goals in life produced results because he was obedient to God.

As I follow God, my goal is to draw near to Him and read my Bible daily. My desire is also to share the love of Christ through my actions and words. I want to experience the prize of knowing Christ more intimately like Paul talks about.

As softball players we should never be satisfied no matter how much success we have had in the past. We should continue to strive to reach higher goals and to always improve our game.

As Christians, we should have goals as well. We can ask God to help us to do everything for His glory. Making this our aim will help us to stay focused on what matters most in life.

"One thing I do, forgetting those things which are behind and reaching forward to those things which are ahead." -Philippians 3:13b

"Trust in the LORD with all your heart, and lean not on your own understanding; In all your ways acknowledge Him, And He shall direct your paths." -Proverbs 3:5-6

Prayer

I want to have the same heart as Paul, God. I want to do everything for Your glory. Keep me from putting earthly goals above the goal of knowing You more intimately. Amen.

Today's Bible Reading: Philippians 3:12-21

Your Story. . . God's Glory

1. In your upcoming season, what are some goals you have for yourself and your team?

2. What goals can you set that involve following God with all your heart?

Day 23

Discipleship

In order for a team to have great success, there must be great leaders within the group. Leaders can possess many different qualities. Some lead by example and work ethic, and others lead by encouragement and selflessness. Some are more vocal while others are quiet, allowing their actions to show their leadership skills.

The best leaders understand the importance of team unity. They take time to build relationships, because they know the team will benefit if they are a close-knit group. Leaders help build a positive environment where everyone feels her role on the team is important. Leaders expect more from themselves and from those around them, and they always believe victory is possible no matter what obstacles they face. Great leaders stay calm when things start to fall apart on the field. These players will often pull the team together on defense after an error is made, helping everyone to regroup and refocus. Exceptional leaders have the respect of their teammates because they lead in a way that makes others want to follow.

I was impacted in a positive way by the leaders on my teams. I became a better player by following their examples, learning from their experiences, and listening to their wisdom. It's just as important for a team to have players who are willing to follow team leaders as it is for a team to have great leadership. When you are surrounded by a teammate who has a good work ethic, quality leadership skills, and good character, you can confidently follow her lead knowing you will benefit.

The Bible talks about the importance of having spiritual leaders, or mentors, in our lives. A mentor is a person who can help you grow in your relationship with Jesus Christ. The person who learns from the mentor is called a disciple in the Bible. Jesus had twelve disciples, or students, that followed Him and learned from Him. Jesus cared first and foremost about the relationship He had with each disciple. He taught them God's truth on a regular basis. Jesus led by example and showed his disciples how to follow God wholeheartedly.

Although I attended church regularly, one of my biggest seasons of growth occurred when I began meeting with a godly woman who agreed to be my mentor. I was excited to learn more about the Bible and sit under her teaching. I felt that I could ask her anything and that nothing was off limits. I appreciated the fact that she answered my questions by sharing what the Bible taught, and not just her opinions or thoughts. She taught me how to be more faithful in prayer. My mentor lived out her faith and was an example to me. To this day, I have a very special relationship with my mentor.

If you have never been mentored, you should start praying for God to put somebody in your life that can encourage you in your faith. As a disciple, you can learn more about who God is, what God has done, who you are, and how you should live. Your knowledge of the Bible will increase, and you will see the benefit of having someone to help you grow.

On the field, we want to follow leaders who motivate and encourage us to become better players and strive for victory. It is easy to follow the example of teammates who have our respect, make good choices, and work hard every day. Off the field, we should choose friends and mentors who will help us to draw closer to Jesus Christ. As we spend time learning as a disciple, God will help us to become who He has created us to be.

"Imitate me, just as I also imitate Christ."
-1 Corinthians 11:1

"And the things that you have heard from me among many witnesses, commit these to faithful men who will be able to teach others also." -2 Timothy 2:2

Prayer

Thank You, Lord, for the mentors in my life. Surround me with mentors who will encourage me in my faith. Help me to grow in Christ and give me opportunities to share Your love with others. Amen.

Today's Bible Reading: 2 Timothy 2

Your Story. . .God's Glory

1. On your current team, are you more of a mentor (a leader who helps others) or a disciple (student still learning the game)?

2. Name two people you consider as your mentors in softball. Share how they have made a difference.

3. Pray and ask God to bring a mentor into your life who can help you grow in your faith. If you already have a mentor, write her name below and share why you are thankful for her.

Day 24

Passion

My gold medals are pretty special to me, but the memories I have from competing with my teammates are even more special. After winning my third gold medal, I knew in my heart it was time to retire; it was here that God began placing a new passion on my heart, and I started to have an unexplainable desire to speak publicly and share my story.

Personally, I did not think I had what it took, but I could not shake this nagging desire. I felt passionate about speaking and could not understand why. The Urban Dictionary defines passion this way: "Passion is when you put more energy into something than is required to do it. It is more than just enthusiasm or excitement, passion is ambition that is materialized into action to put as much heart, mind, body, and soul into something as possible." I experienced these feelings when I played softball, but now I was feeling this similar ambition towards speaking, and I didn't even feel like I was good at it. This is how I knew it was from God. I would not have chosen this direction for myself.

During this time, I was drawing close to God and asking for His will to be done in my life. I prayed and told God that I would go wherever He led and would speak whatever He placed upon my heart to share. Shortly afterward, I had opportunities to speak at softball clinics and other events around the country. As I shared about my Olympic journey and my faith, I felt like I wasn't very good at speaking. But, each time after I finished my speech, people came up to me and shared how my story encouraged them. God used what they said to give me peace that I was doing exactly what He called me to do.

When I think back to when I started playing softball as a little girl, I knew I had fallen in love with the game because I always wanted to have a ball in my hand. I played catch with my friend whenever I went over her house.

I enjoyed sticking around the field after our games and throwing the ball around for hours because I couldn't get enough of it. I looked forward to my pitching lessons and putting in the time practicing what I learned when I left.

When you have a passion for what you are doing, it doesn't feel like hard work. You get enjoyment from the process. You see the benefit of the repetition and monotonous drills at practice. When you're committed, you are willing to get through the hard times, learn from the mistakes, and strive to get better at what you are doing. If you are passionate about the sport of softball, you know that all the sacrifices you are making and the time you are putting in to improve your skills are worth it.

But what does it look like to have a passion for God? When we are passionate about our faith, we commit to spending time learning the Bible, we pray often, we attend church regularly, we help others, and we allow God to work in our lives. We make Jesus the priority! When we do this, God will allow us to use our talents and put our passion into action.

Staying passionate about Jesus—first and foremost—is a constant challenge in the busy lives we lead. This is why we must ask God to help us to follow Him closely while surrounding ourselves with friends who love Jesus. This will help to keep us accountable. It will also help us to be used by God to impact others. Love the Lord your God with all your heart, and be ready for Him to use your passions for His glory.

"Jesus said to him, 'You shall love the LORD your God with all your heart, with all your soul, and with all your mind.'" -Matthew 22:37

"So he answered and said, 'You shall love the LORD your God with all your heart, with all your soul, with all your strength, and with all your mind,' and 'your neighbor as yourself.'" -Luke 10:27

Prayer

Jesus, help me to be passionate in my pursuit of You. And thank You for the opportunity to display my passion on the softball field. Help me to acknowledge You in all I do and to follow the path You have chosen for me. Amen.

Today's Bible Reading: Deuteronomy 6:1-9

Your Story. . .God's Glory

1. Write down the top five things you are passionate about in life or that mean the most to you.

2. What steps can you take to help you put God first in your life and live out the command for you to love the Lord with all your heart?

Day 25

Support System

I leaned forward as my name was called, and an Olympic official placed the gold medal around my neck. In that moment, my dream had come true. Team USA was the top team in the world and was the first ever to win gold in the sport of softball at the 1996 Olympic Games. Immediately, I turned toward the stands where my mom, dad, sister, brother, and 11-month-old nephew were standing and cheering. With tears in my eyes and a smile on my face, I waved to them.

I knew the support I received from my family was the main reason I was on that podium with my teammates. I could not have won a gold medal without their help. My parents signed me up to play softball when I was six years old. They sacrificed a lot to afford pitching lessons for me. They selflessly drove me around to practices and games. Even our tournaments and national championships turned into family vacations because they supported my passion. My dad coached me in youth league and travel ball. My mom cheered the loudest for me and was there to comfort me when I needed it most. Their encouragement helped me to go after my dreams of winning a National Championship and earning a college scholarship.

Besides my parents, I had support from my siblings, coaches, teammates, and friends. There are many people who impact us in our softball journeys. Our coaches teach us fundamental skills and game strategies. They believe in us and push us to be our best. Our teammates help us to learn how to work together with others. Our friends cheer us on as well. Multiple people have played important roles in helping us to become who we are today.

As athletes, the spotlight is on us, but it is important to acknowledge and thank the people who are behind us. You have people who care for you and make it possible for you to play this great sport. Each time you take the field, think about the fact that somebody has helped transport you to and from your practice or game. Remind yourself of the coaches who have helped you get better and the teammates who are learning along with you. Thank these people for their support and help.

God places people in our lives for a reason. Each coach, teammate, family member, friend, opponent, and umpire can make an impact in our lives. Through our relationships and experiences, God gives us opportunities to live in ways that honor Him. We learn to listen and follow instructions from our coaches.

We experience tough losses and thrilling victories, but we get to do it with teammates who battle next to us. We are able to turn to family for comfort in the hardest losses. We should respect our opponents and act with class no matter the outcome of the game. And we must learn to have self-control when reacting over calls made by umpires, especially when we disagree with calls they make. God uses people and our interactions with them to build and reveal our character.

Many spiritual lessons are learned on a softball field. We have opportunities to show humility, patience, and kindness. We find ourselves in situations where we can treat others the way we want to be treated. As God's children, we need to forgive teammates who hurt our feelings.

We should put others first and pray for the people around us. We are called to live above the drama that sometimes happens on teams. We get to share the love of Christ that He offers to everyone through our actions and words. Playing a team sport brings many opportunities to practice biblical qualities.

Let's get in God's Word and ask Him to help us in all of these areas—our God will help us every single time, even when we fail. When you use your position on your team to be an example to others, your light will shine, and people will see God working in you and give Him glory. Through the support of those around you, you can live out God's perfect plan for your life.

"Let your light so shine before men, that they may see your good works and glorify your Father in heaven."
-Matthew 5:16

"Therefore comfort each other and edify one another, just as you also are doing." -1 Thessalonians 5:11

Prayer

Dear God, thank You for the support system in my life. Thank You for the coaches and teammates on my team. Please work in my life, and help me to be humble, forgiving, kind, and encouraging to others. Amen.

Today's Bible Reading: Galatians 5:13-26

Your Story. . .God's Glory

1. Who are the biggest supporters in your softball career?

2. How does it feel when you win with your teammates? What about when you lose?

3. In what ways can you let your light shine and glorify God to those around you?

Day 26

Identity

How we view ourselves and where we look to find our identity is something every one of us should consider. Collins English Dictionary explains a person's identity as "the characteristics that distinguish them from others."

Many people are constantly focused on things like: trying to fit in, being accepted, having popularity on social media, finding success on the softball field, or chasing after earthly possessions. They classify themselves by what they do, what they have, or even what relationships they are in, but that is not who they truly are.

We must be careful not to fall into the trap of a false identity. The world is constantly telling us who we are or who we should be. Most of the time, the titles we hold are defined by what we do or do not accomplish.

Somebody might say, what is wrong with wanting to be identified as a softball player?

I experienced the ups and downs that go with that type of thinking. When things are going well, it is nice to feel that you have more value and worth because of your performance on the field. But, as soon as the game starts to get harder and you go into a slump or start to make errors on the field, your emotions tend to sink as well. If an injury sidelines you, you might feel depressed because you are not able to play. Suddenly, you might think you do not have value because you are known for being a softball player. Sometimes having an injury causes an athlete to question who she really is because her identity has been wrapped up in her play on the field.

This can be a dangerous thought process.

We are all striving for perfection, but the more we tie our worth to our performance, the more likely we are to experience anxiety, depression, or other negative emotions.

Even with success, tying our worth to our accomplishments is not healthy. People might look at me as a three-time Olympic gold medalist and think they wouldn't mind that as their identity. But, there can be expectations tied to success. All of a sudden, we might try to be someone we are not because someone else views us in a way we can't live up to. Or, people might become full of pride and think of themselves higher than they ought to—the Bible warns us against this.

My gold medals are accomplishments that I'm very proud of. But, these accomplishments are only a way for me to share with others who I am. We only find out who we truly are when we realize "whose" we are. When God is your Father, you begin to learn that your identity is found in Christ alone. Jesus died for you and made you into a new creation when you asked Him to be the Lord of your life. Your identity in Christ is eternal and will never change no matter what you accomplish in life or how often you fall short of your goals.

This should be encouraging because we can be free from having to prove that we are worthy in God's eyes. God loves us unconditionally no matter what. Once I realized this, I started to be able to look at the game of softball from a different perspective. I still didn't like to fail, but my emotions weren't so tied to my performance; I understood I was treasured by God and set apart for His glory—and the truth is, you are too if you love Jesus!

In fact, 1 Peter 2:9 says, "But you are a chosen generation, a royal priesthood, a holy nation, His own special people, that you may proclaim the praises of Him who called you out of darkness into His marvelous light."

This is who God says you are. It's your job to believe God and take Him at His Word. The next time you start to think you are not good enough or that your value comes from your performance that day on the field, remember what God says about you. You are His child and He loves you.

In fact, you are more than a conqueror through Christ who loves you.

"Therefore, if anyone is in Christ, he is a new creation; old things have passed away; behold, all things have become new." -2 Corinthians 5:17

"I will praise You, for I am fearfully and wonderfully made; marvelous are Your works, and that my soul knows very well." -Psalm 139:14

Prayer

Please forgive me, Lord, for finding my identity and value in my accomplishments. Teach me how to keep my identity in Christ at all times. Your Word says that I am new creation. Help me to live for You. Amen.

Today's Bible Reading: Colossians 3:1-17

Your Story. . .God's Glory

1. Share some thoughts on how you view yourself and where you look to find your identity, value, worth, or acceptance.

2. Do you ever tie your value or worth to your accomplishments? If so, why do you think you do this?

3. Write down Psalm 139:14 below. Do you believe this biblical truth? Why or why not?

Day 27

Share Your Knowledge

I took the field in Athens, Greece, and ran to my position at first base. This was my third Olympic games. My teammates and I trained harder than ever before to bring home the gold medal once again. USA Softball had been the top-ranked team in the world for years, and we wanted to keep that title. We dominated all week long and made it to the championship game against a strong Australian team filled with veterans. We scored three runs in the first inning, and by the seventh inning we had a 5-1 lead.

We took the field...we were just three outs away from winning the gold medal, and I was trying to keep my emotions in check. The softball clock was ticking, and the end of my career was minutes away. One out. Two outs. A pitch was thrown, the Australian batter hit the ball— a ground ball to the left side of the field. I went back to the bag, turned, and caught the ball thrown on a line from our shortstop. The final out was made! We threw our hands in the air and screamed with excitement. Every player ran toward the center of the field, and we celebrated with a dog pile near the pitcher's circle. That celebration was nothing compared to the feeling I experienced as I stood on the podium and received the gold medal around my neck—my third, and last, gold medal.

I retired after the 2004 Athens Olympics.

Since then, I have traveled the country speaking, working with softball players of all ages, and sharing my gold medals. I let people hold and wear all three gold medals around their necks. The medals have scratches all over them from being shared so often. One of my medals has a couple dents in it from being dropped on accident by an excited elementary school student. There are more finger prints on my medals than you can count. What has been special is the reaction and emotion from people as they experience putting the gold medals around their necks. These medals are meant to be shared in my opinion. As special as they are to me, I get more joy when I share them.

This is how I feel about my relationship with God. It is meant to be shared and to be experienced with others. As I share Jesus with others, some people hear about hope for the first time. Those who have placed their trust in Jesus are encouraged in what they already believe. Others realize they no longer have to feel shame or guilt because Jesus died to free them from all of that.

Many will hear God's truth and feel like a weight is lifted off their shoulders because they no longer have to strive to be good enough—they just need to turn to Jesus and allow Him to work in their lives. Some people don't believe in God, and some believe in different gods from other religions. As a Christian, I can be an example by sharing love and God's truth with everyone no matter how different our beliefs are.

My medals, along with all my earthly possessions, are fading and won't go to heaven with me when I die. This reminds me to keep a proper perspective of the game of softball when I start to become wrapped up in feeling my worth and value comes from what I do on the field. Softball is a game, heaven is eternal. My medals will rust, my faith in Christ will last forever.

With my eyes on Jesus, and heaven as my promise, I live life fully.

These gold medals won't compare to the streets of gold in heaven (Revelation 21:21). Nothing will compare to seeing God face-to-face. I look forward to what awaits me when I take my last breath in this life and instantly enter eternity with God. I might not be able to take my medals with me, but the people who I shared Christ with and who accepted Him as Lord will be there. That is what I think about when I think about what matters most.

"...that the sharing of your faith may become effective by the acknowledgement of every good thing which is in you in Christ Jesus." -Philemon 1:6

"For I am not ashamed of the gospel of Christ, for it is the power of God to salvation for everyone who believes." -Romans 1:16a

Prayer

Jesus, give me the confidence to share Your love and truth with other people. Keep me from being embarrassed or worried about what other people will think. I pray for all the people I care about to trust in You and receive eternal life. Amen.

Today's Bible Reading: Revelation 21

Your Story. . .God's Glory

1. What do you and your friends/teammates talk about the most?

2. Have you ever shared about Jesus Christ and His love with others? If so, describe your experience.

3. Pray and ask God for the courage to share about Jesus with one friend this week.

Day 28

Perseverance

Starting at the age of six, I was blessed to play what I consider to be one of the most competitive and passionate sports—softball! Through this amazing game, I was able to compete and be a part of many winning teams filled with incredible athletes. I was blessed to play, not only throughout the United States, but also around the world representing our great country.

But it was never easy.

I had to persevere, practice, make sacrifices, listen to my coaches, and stay focused on my goal of competing at the highest level; all while applying everything I could to the sport that I loved, each and every day. It was through this commitment, that I became part of some very successful teams, winning three NCAA Division I national championships in Oklahoma City with the University of Arizona softball team (1993, 1994, 1997) and three gold medals in three Olympics (1996, 2000, 2004).

Do you desire to be all that you can be in this sport that God has given you a talent for? Do you aspire to succeed and play at the collegiate or professional level? Do you dream of playing in the Olympics one day? If so, it is going to have to be your decision to stay focused and never give up.

Take the story of Hannah in 1 Samuel 1 & 2. She had a desire. She had a passion—and God put within Hannah a desire that was hers alone. She wanted a baby boy.

But, for years it didn't happen.

However, Hannah knew God. She understood His power and knew that with Him, nothing was impossible.

Hannah prayed.

She persevered and petitioned. She sought the Lord, staying determined and focused.

Heartbroken...she prayed.

Feeling hopeless...she prayed.

Weeping and crying...she prayed.

In Hannah's greatest moments of weakness, God became her strength! He honored her prayers with a boy named Samuel, who wrote 1 & 2 Samuel, and was very influential in the work of God for Israel.

Never give up on your dream to play your favorite sport. Never stop praying for something in your life that is only possible with God's help. Use the story of Hannah and her son, Samuel, as a reminder that God can answer your prayers. Walk purposefully and passionately in all that God has gifted you with.

Remember that all things are possible with our Heavenly Father. We can do all things in the name of our Savior, Jesus Christ.

"I can do all things through Christ who strengthens me."
-Philippians 4:13

"So it came to pass in the process of time that Hannah conceived and bore a son, and called his name Samuel, saying, 'Because I have asked for him from the Lord.'" -1 Samuel 1:20

Prayer

Help me to call out to You in my weakness, Lord. When things don't go how I expect, help me to persevere in prayer and trust You with all my heart. I know You will answer my prayers according to Your perfect will. Amen.

Today's Bible Reading: 1 Samuel 1

Your Story. . .God's Glory

1. In what ways have you had to persevere in softball? What challenges have you had to face?

2. Do you have a dream or desire in your heart for your future? Write your thoughts below.

Day 29

Overcoming Trials

I came around third base and was headed home. The catcher was receiving the ball as I was about to slide at the plate. I quickly made the decision to go around the outside of her body and reached for home plate with my left arm completely extended. She missed my body when she went to tag me out, and I was safe.

Immediately, I felt pain in my left shoulder. We were a couple months out from the Olympic Games. Luckily, my injury was not very serious and only kept me out for a short time as I rehabbed my arm until it was completely healed. I have had other teammates who have not been as fortunate and have been injured at an important time in their careers.

I think of my teammate who sprained her ankle and it swelled up as big as a softball the day before the Women's College World Series started our freshman year. She had to sit out the majority of the tournament, and although she could barely walk, she entered the final game at shortstop. She played in pain because she wanted to be on that field to help our team more than anything. Injuries are a part of the game. They are never timely and always bring frustration and sadness.

I have seen a renewed purpose in athletes who have come back from injuries that took them out of competition for any period of time. Going through a trial can give athletes a new perspective and can make them more thankful for the opportunity to compete after having to sit out.

Injuries cause players to persevere as they work to rebuild their strength. They get tested mentally and physically. Injuries make players learn patience because it is not a choice for them to be out of the game. Many times there will be more of a passion to play once someone has been injured.

James 1:2-4 says, "...count it all joy when you fall into various trials, knowing that the testing of your faith produces patience. But let patience have its perfect work, that you may be perfect and complete, lacking nothing." This can be hard to understand.

Injuries are just one type of trial we might go through in sports. We also might have trials with our teammates, struggle to play well, or have times of feeling like we are not good enough.

How can God expect us to find joy in our trials? Because He knows what can come from a trial. When we are tested, our faith is shown by how we respond. Do you remember earlier in this study when I talked about "getting bitter or getting better"? Do we turn to God or do we blame Him? God can use trials to teach us lessons and to allow us to live out genuine faith. I have seen perseverance and steadfastness in people as they work to overcome adversity. Through the struggle, patience brings about maturity.

When the results from hard times produce this maturity, often people become stronger, physically and spiritually, than they were prior to their difficulty. God will use trials in our lives to show us where we must look when things get hard. The right place to turn is to Jesus Christ. Anywhere else will not bring us to the place that God has chosen, where we are lacking nothing.

"And not only that, but we also glory in tribulations, knowing that tribulation produces perseverance; and perseverance, character; and character, hope."
-Romans 5:3-4

"For I, the LORD your God, will hold your right hand, saying to you, 'Fear not, I will help you.'" -Isaiah 41:13

Prayer

Dear God, help me to learn and grow from the trials in my life. I need Your strength to persevere. Help me to allow You to build my character in the hard times. I never want to lose sight of the hope that I have in Jesus Christ. Amen.

Today's Bible Reading: James 1:2-18

Your Story. . .God's Glory

1. Have you had any injuries that have kept you out of playing softball? If so, how did you react, and what did you learn from your situation?

2. Did you come back from your injury with renewed purpose? Explain.

3. Where do you turn when you go through a hard time–to God or somewhere else? Why?

Day 30
Sacrifice

In college, I spent a lot of time batting second in the lineup. I enjoyed that spot because I knew I was hitting behind a quick runner. When the leadoff hitter got on base, my job was to lay down a sacrifice bunt in order to move the runner into scoring position.

In the closest games, I knew one run could be the difference between winning and losing; therefore, I took my job of getting the sacrifice bunt down very seriously. I saw how the successful execution of a sacrifice bunt led to more offensive opportunities. These types of productive outs helped our team to score more runs, which in turn led to many victories.

Not everyone likes it when their coach calls on them to put down the sacrifice bunt. In fact, I have heard players say they pretend they don't know the sign or get frustrated when the coach gives them the bunt signal. Sometimes it's because they don't have confidence in their bunting abilities, and other times it's because they would prefer to hit away, regardless of the game situation.

There can be a battle in our minds between doing what we want to do and doing what is best for the team. How we respond can be the difference between winning and losing a game. Our decisions also show whether we put our desires first or the needs of the team first.

There is another way the word "sacrifice" is experienced in the sport of softball. Through the commitment to our team, we make a lot of sacrifices to play. For instance, if we have practice during the week, we sacrifice time with our family and friends. If we have a lot of homework after practice, we sacrifice sleep by staying up late to finish our work. Sometimes due to our softball schedule, we miss birthday parties, school functions, church events, or even vacations.

I know a lot of families struggle with missing church during softball season because the schedule can be so demanding. When your practice or game is held on the same day and time as your church service, you have to make the tough choice to keep your commitment to your team or miss practice or the game. I struggled with this balance when I played on Sunday mornings in college. Eventually, I learned to live out my faith on the field no matter what day of the week it was.

I wrote a Bible verse on my glove. I prayed with my teammates before our games. When I signed autographs for our fans, I wrote a verse next to my name. I made sacrifices to play at the elite level, but I was also able to be used by God in ways I wouldn't have been able to if I wasn't on the team.

I encourage you to view the softball field as a place where you can live out your faith. When you step out onto the field, thank God for the opportunity to play with the talent that He has blessed you with. Ask God to help you to be a godly example to your teammates through your words and actions. Offer to pray before the game with your teammates. Know that God has you on your team for a reason.

When I learned that I could worship God through my sport and play for His glory, I had a new view regarding my purpose on my team. You might not be able to be in church every Sunday, but you can bring church to the field. There might be players who have never been to church before, and you can be an example to them.

When we are reminded that God has a plan for our lives and understand that He can even use us on the softball field, we will know that the sacrifices we are making can bring great rewards.

"Greater love has no one than this, than to lay down one's life for his friends." -John 15:13

"By this we know love, because He laid down His life for us. And we also ought to lay down our lives for the brethren." -1 John 3:16

Prayer

Jesus, thank You for the sacrifice You made for me when You died upon the cross. You conquered death when You rose from the grave. Help me to recognize the bigger picture when I have to make a sacrifice. Help me to lay down my life for my friends. Amen.

Today's Bible Reading: 1 Corinthians 13

Your Story. . .God's Glory

1. What sacrifices have you made to play softball?

2. Do you struggle with having to miss church because your softball schedule interferes?

3. What are two things you can do to bring "church" to your team? (e.g.: pray with teammates, put a Bible verse in the dugout, share about a devotion you read, etc.)

Day 31

Ultimate Victory

My first national championship tournament in travel ball was held in Chattanooga, Tennessee. I was fourteen years old, and I was nervous and excited at the same time. With fifty-two teams competing from all over the country, this was the biggest tournament I had ever played in before.

We made it all the way to the championship. I was the starting pitcher in the game. Our team battled hard, and we finished on top. I had won local tournaments before, but this one felt different. This was the point when my dream to play softball in college began. I tasted victory and knew this was something I wanted to experience again.

Being the champion at the end of the season is an amazing feeling. Hard work, dedication, obstacles, sacrifice, life lessons, and commitment are all part of the journey. The memories and relationships you walk away with will stay with you forever.

When you end your season with a victory, it makes the entire experience that much better. The Bible talks about a different kind of victory. It talks about the victory we have in Jesus Christ, each and every day.

In 1 John 5:3-5, it says that if we love God, we will obey His commands and those commands will not be a burden to us. It also tells us that our faith gives us victory because we are overcomers if we believe that Jesus Christ is the Son of God who came to earth to save us from our sins.

Don't ever forget: Every child of God has victory—through faith in Jesus Christ.

We all have our own unique stories, and I hope as you have read this devotional, you have been reminded that God is writing your story. As you continue to follow Him, He will guide you down the path created just for you.

You are an overcomer if you have faith in Jesus. So, choose today to live with the confidence of knowing God will work together all things in your life for good (Romans 8:28). When things don't go how you want or when things get hard, keep trusting God because He is faithful! He will carry you through your struggles.

If victory on a softball field is sweet, think of how much sweeter the victory will be when we experience heaven one day. Jesus told us that even when we have trouble in this world, we should be encouraged because He has overcome the world (John 16:33).

With Jesus in your life, you can overcome any trial you face.

Seek Jesus with all your heart and surrender everything in your life to Him. He promises to be your strength in weakness, your help in times of trouble, your hope in times of worry, and your joy in times of uncertainty.

We are not meant to live out our faith alone. Just as we experience the thrill of victory with our teammates, when we are surrounded by people who love Jesus, we will be encouraged in our faith as well.

When we win a softball tournament, our prize is a ring, trophy, or medal. These type of prizes, although meaningful, are perishable and will fade over time. This is not the case with our faith. God has an imperishable crown waiting for all who love Him (1 Corinthians 9:24-25). The victory is yours!

"Now thanks be to God who always leads us in triumph in Christ, and through us diffuses the fragrance of His knowledge in every place." -2 Corinthians 2:14

"What then shall we say to these things? If God is for us, who can be against us? He who did not spare His own Son, but delivered Him up for us all, how shall He not with Him also freely give us all things?" -Romans 8:31-32

Prayer

Jesus, You are my very great reward. I know I have victory because You are the Lord of my life. Please surround me with people who will help me stay focused on living for Your glory. Amen.

Today's Bible Reading: 1 Corinthians 9:24-27

Your Story. . .God's Glory

1. What is the greatest victory you have experienced in softball?

2. What can you do to make sure you finish strong in your journey of faith and stay focused on Jesus Christ until the end?

"The Catch"

(Day 14 Devotional)

CONNECT WITH LEAH

I hope you enjoyed this devotional. I am passionate about wanting softball players of all ages to experience the confidence, hope, and joy that come from a personal relationship with Jesus Christ. The sport of softball gave me lifelong friendships, lessons, and memories. Even more than that, I am most thankful for God revealing Himself to me in a powerful way when I was a student-athlete in college. My life was never the same once I chose to follow Jesus. We train hard as athletes. Let's make the choice to pursue Christ more fervently than we pursue our goals on the field. Let's read God's Word daily so we can know truth. When we obey and follow God, we can be confident that we are living right in the middle of God's perfect plan and will for our lives.

I'd love to connect with you on social media. Share pictures holding your devotional book, or let me know how God is working in your life as you read through it. Share your stories from the softball fields also.

Make sure to use this hashtag: #softballglorygodsstory

Twitter: @leah20usa

Instagram: @leah20usa

Website: www.leah20.com

God Bless You

Made in the USA
Las Vegas, NV
09 November 2022

59048697R00075